CW01506567

The Year of the Dog

Also by Sophia Money-Coutts

How One Tiny Terrier Ruined My
Sofa but Saved My Life

the
year
of the
dog

Sophia
Money-Coutts

ONE PLACE. MANY STORIES

HQ
An imprint of HarperCollins*Publishers* Ltd
1 London Bridge Street
London SE1 9GF

www.harpercollins.co.uk

HarperCollins*Publishers*
Macken House, 39/40 Mayor Street Upper,
Dublin 1, D01 C9W8, Ireland

This edition 2025
1
First published in Great Britain by HQ,
an imprint of HarperCollins*Publishers* Ltd 2025

Sophia Money-Coutts asserts the moral right to be identified as the author of
this work.
A catalogue record for this book is available from the British Library.

ISBN: 978-0-00-874403-8

This book is set in 10.7/15.5 pt. Sabon by Type-it AS, Norway

This novel is entirely a work of fiction. The names, characters and incidents
portrayed in it are the work of the author's imagination. Any resemblance to
actual persons, living or dead, events or localities is entirely coincidental.

Printed and bound in the UK using 100% Renewable
Electricity by CPI Group (UK) Ltd

For more information visit: www.harpercollins.co.uk/green

To Dennis (who, perhaps fortunately, cannot read)

Introduction

'I don't think there is a right time,' Mike said one evening, as we cooked dinner in my kitchen. 'I think it's like children, you just have to do it.'

He and I had been together for six months, having met on a dating app towards the end of 2023. On our first date, we went for a walk along a North London towpath and soon after fell in love. Wild, mad, magical love. He left hidden Post-it notes in my bedroom; we went for long walks, hand in hand, trying to impress one another with talk of our favourite books. Going to Sainsbury's to buy milk and loo roll felt romantic. It *was* romantic, his hand on the small of my back as we queued for a self-service checkout while I clutched a pack of Andrex.

I'd spent most of my twenties and thirties looking for my person while it felt like, all around me, other people had already met theirs. Not long after I'd turned 30, when I was heartbroken after the end of another relationship, one of my oldest friends came to my office and took me out for lunch. 'I'm pregnant!' Lou announced, and as I trudged back down Oxford Street afterwards, mixed emotions rolling around inside me like marbles, I counted the number of steps she was ahead of me on my fingers:

1. She'd met someone.
2. They'd gone out for long enough to get engaged.
3. They'd bought a flat together.
4. They'd got married.
5. They were now having a baby.

Life wasn't a competition, I told myself, everyone's on their own timetable. But, still, what was wrong with me? There must be something wrong with me. When would it be my turn?

I hated the part of me that felt like this.

I spent the rest of my thirties going to hen parties and weddings. I sung 'I Vow To Thee My Country' 932 times and dutifully bought John Lewis towels and glasses from the wedding lists. Sometimes, a friend would bring their new partner to whichever Home Counties wedding we were going to that weekend and I'd think jealously, 'They'll be next.' Because it never felt like it was going to be me.

Tortoise-like, I pulled in my head and developed a shell around me as a defence mechanism. Maybe I didn't even want to get married. Maybe I didn't want to have children. Why have women been dancing the same steps for so long? We weren't wearing bonnets anymore. Putting on a white dress and standing in church when nobody even believed in religion was old-fashioned, anyway. Did you know, I became fond of telling people, that marriage shortens a woman's life span by a year and a half? (I tried not to mention this interesting fact at actual weddings.)

I told myself these things because to admit otherwise was to allow that I felt left behind by my friends and my siblings, all marrying off. After so long of feeling like a reject, it felt more powerful if I rejected these modern benchmarks of social success – an engagement picture on Instagram, a profile picture in a wedding dress, the first hospital photo with your new baby. I didn't need a man or a wedding. I would work. I would travel. I would look after myself.

And then I met Mike, a tall, handsome, softly spoken man who I first saw sitting on a bench beside the canal, reading a book, early for our first date. He was proudly bohemian, I quickly learned – an academic who studied medical genetics and lived at the top of a converted factory in East London, overlooking the canal. He was clever, funny, wildly charming, and when he smiled at me it was like feeling the sun on my face.

I was 38 and he was 52 and had been married before, but this meant he communicated like a grown-up – honestly and openly – which made me feel like I could be more honest and open than I'd been in previous relationships. There was a sense of calm between us, as if we'd both found one another after a long storm and knew things were now going to be OK. Suddenly, the idea of marriage didn't seem old-fashioned. Suddenly, the idea of committing to someone made sense. 'He feels like a brother already,' my sister Rosie whispered to me after meeting him for the first time. Maybe my turn had come round. Maybe I could even have a baby.

Around the same time that Mike and I started seeing one

another, my mother was diagnosed with a brain tumour. My brave, stoic, uncomplaining mum had already suffered three rounds of ovarian cancer, and now it had wormed its way to her brain. Because she lived by herself, in a cottage at the end of a farm track in Sussex, Rosie and I took turns to drive down from London for hospital trips and moral support. Mum had a naughty terrier called Beano to keep her company, but he wasn't so good at driving or cooking.

It was a strange but very present time, falling in love while trying to get my head around the idea that my mother might soon not be here. My head was a tumble dryer of emotions – fear, joy, panic, euphoria, sheer disbelief that a person could exist in this world one minute and vanish the next. I didn't think much beyond each week because I wasn't sure what that week would look like.

All in all, it probably wasn't the ideal time to start discussing a puppy.

Just before we met, Mike had decided he'd tired of dating and would get a dog instead. I was the last roll of the dice, he joked. I'd long thought about getting a dog too. I'd grown up with them – a succession of terriers, Labradors, vizslas and mongrels – but worried that I travelled too much.

With Mike, it seemed more feasible. Something we could share. The question of moving in together and children was hanging in the air, but, in the meantime, a dog.

I lived in a big flat in leafy South-East London. It had a large garden with a den of foxes at the back of it, squirrels that skipped along the fences and parakeets that screeched overhead. The perfect place for a dog. Also, I was a freelance writer working from home all day, writing in bed or on the kitchen sofa or at my desk, depending on my mood. It could be lonely, all day at my laptop. It *was* lonely sometimes, before Mike. But a dog would be my companion. We could go to the nearby park when I got stuck halfway through a sentence, which happens quite a lot.

Mike was already signed up to various animal rescue charities, and we lay entwined in bed, scrolling through pictures. How about this one? Or that one? Should we adopt a street dog from Romania?

'How about we each get a puppy from the same litter?' I suggested.

'What if we broke up?' Mike said. 'They wouldn't see one another.'

I laughed because that was impossible.

He favoured a spaniel; I quite wanted a terrier of some sort. A little, fierce dog. And then, online, I spotted a litter of parson terrier puppies in a small town just outside Birmingham.

Parson terriers are like big Jack Russells – some smooth-coated, some fluffier. Cartoon dogs, some call them, because they look a bit like Snowy from *Tintin*. Mum has had two parsons – Trumpet, and his successor, Beano – so I knew about them. They're funny, clever, stubborn, and will shred a soft toy within five minutes of being given one. They're sworn enemies of all squirrels, and endlessly loyal.

I messaged Lorraine, the breeder, asking to come and see the litter. I'd seen a picture of a small boy with brown and black splotches like a world map on his back who looked like he might be my dog. Mike was having a tricky time with a research project, so I said I'd forge ahead with the puppy plan and he could act as support. The puppy would technically be mine but, really, ours.

On a sunny day in May, I drove up north and parked in a farm-steading. Inside the house was a pen, and inside that pen were six furry puppies. Just six weeks old. All asleep on top of one another, like fat maggots. Lorraine reached into the pen and plucked out the boy with the world map on his back.

I'd visited one litter prior to this and held a small girl who was very sweet, with a black face and a tail that curled over her back. But she wasn't my dog. This little guy – with his white paws, floppy brown ears and little dark eyes that squinted at me – he was mine. I gently laid him down on Lorraine's kitchen floor and knelt, whereupon he waddled up to my knees and pounced towards my outstretched hand with a baby growl. He was the one.

Quickly, I told Lorraine I wanted him, transferred the deposit, and got back in the car. I WhatsApped Mike a video and a few photos.

'Oh my darling, he's perfect!' he replied. 'I love him!'

'We can pick him up in a month,' I replied happily, before pulling out of the farm and heading south again.

I'd bought a puppy. A puppy who would save me, although I didn't know that yet.

June

Things I google in June:

- best toys for puppies
- dog playpen
- dog bed reviews
- charles dickens dog names
- how many calories brazil nut
- puppy sleep in bedroom or kitchen
- is princess anne more senior to princess of wales
- puppy just ate a gaviscon is that ok
- puppy hiccups
- why is my puppy licking his willy so much
- what age can puppy go through night
- puppy three poos a day too many
- best dog poo bags
- is my puppy too fat
- bromley bin collection what day

1 JUNE

I've decided on a name. Dennis. Partly because this links him to Mum's dog (Beano), partly because he looks like a Dennis. Mike preferred 'Monty', because he's always quoting from *Withnail and I*, but I feel like Monty is the name for a fat Labrador.

A nice woman called Gail Garbutt has sent me her book on dog names after I mentioned that I was getting a puppy in my weekly Substack newsletter. She must be quite a posh woman, because some of the suggestions include naming your dog after a Scottish river (Oykel or Beauly) or shipping stations (Biscay or Humber). There's also a funny list of food suggestions, but I couldn't imagine standing in Crystal Palace Park and bellowing 'Crouton' or 'Chutney' at the top of my voice. I'd be arrested.

6 JUNE

Picked up a crate from a woman who lives nearby. I found her on Facebook Marketplace. When I knocked on her door, there was loud barking inside. 'Beware of the dog!' said a sign on her gate. Sounded more like a lion.

'Ignore him. Hades wouldn't hurt a fly,' said the woman, emerging with the crate under her arm. She dropped it at her feet with a great crash. 'Needs a hose down,' she announced, as I surveyed its rusty bars and thick covering of cobwebs. 'But otherwise, good as new.'

I felt like one of those expectant mothers deliberating over an expensive new pram or buying a second-hand one. Dennis will be alright in this, I told myself, once I'd cleaned and disinfected it. I handed over a £20 note, shoved it into my car, and quickly reversed as the barking continued inside.

Hades was not in the posh dog names book.

9 JUNE

'Two weeks today!' I text Mike. Two weeks from today, we drive north to pick up Dennis.

He sends back a row of dog and heart-face emojis.

I keep piling new puppy toys and related accessories that I've ordered online onto the desk in my sitting room. The pile now includes several chew toys, a packet of tennis balls, a bottle of enzymatic spray to protect my carpets, a bumper pack of puppy pads, several bags of dog treats, a toy sheep, a toy pig, a toy fox and a toy rabbit.

15 JUNE

In Sussex with Mum. Drove her to the hardware shop because she still hasn't got her driving licence back after the operation to remove her tumour, and she needed supplies for her bird table.

While she inspected bags of seed, I deliberated over poo bags. Scented or non-scented? Compostable? With handles or without? In the end, I went for a box of 'extra strong' ones. Strength feels like the most important quality in a poo bag.

Go home and watch *Corrie* on the sofa. Dee-Dee the lawyer has agreed to marry Joel, which Mum reckons will be a disaster. Funny how, before her diagnosis, I used to resent having to sit through it whenever I visited. Now, I couldn't be more grateful for the normality – quiet evening on the sofa, glass of wine and bowl of crisps between us. Lovely, lovely normality.

Show Mum the latest video from Lorraine of Dennis scampering about her garden with his siblings, fat little dumplings pouncing on one another. Dennis leaves the pack for a few moments to try to jump up on a garden chair but he's too small, so he tries again and falls back on the grass, then again with the same result. 'Very independent,' Mum remarks, approvingly.

16 JUNE

Didn't know there was such controversy over dog food. Apparently feeding them kibble is akin to giving them Jammy Dodgers because it's so processed and can contain nasty bits of animal, including eyeballs. According to a book by dog-mad journalist India Knight, raw food is better because it's what dogs would have originally eaten when lolloping around the plains in the wild.

She was persuaded about its benefits after learning about a man who fed his dog raw food and once put a poo bag in his pocket during a walk, then forgot about it for a few days because the poo was so small, firm and odourless. 'Come on,' she writes in her book, in disbelief. 'This man is lying. He is a dirty liar from Liarsville.' But apparently he wasn't.

Spend some time researching this online, then order a crate of raw puppy mince. It's mixed with organic kale, organic seaweed, organic broccoli, pumpkin seeds, blackberries and nettles and costs £57 for a month's supply. I'm not entirely convinced that dogs would have eaten organic seaweed and kale in the wild, but at least he'll be getting his five a day.

17 JUNE

Order a small dog blanket online and get it delivered to Lorraine to put in the bed with Dennis, his siblings and his mother. I've read that this helps them settle into their new home because it acts as a comfort blanket, something that smells familiar when they've been separated. Mustn't think about taking Dennis away from his mum forever because it makes me well up. He's going to have a lovely time in London with 900 toys and the diet of a weight-lifter.

18 JUNE

Set up the crate in the corner of the kitchen and put a puppy pad and an old blanket inside it. Also, the toy pig. Send Mike a photo of the crate as proudly as if I'd created a nursery.

20 JUNE

My friend Emily texts from Florida: 'Are you ready? Puppies are more work than babies, fyi.' She has a toddler and a golden retriever called Mowgli, but I think she must be fibbing.

22 JUNE

Erect a pen on a small patch of grass in the garden, then spray it with purple disinfectant so Dennis can scamper about this area of lawn until his jabs have kicked in. Feel bad for the worms but I keep reading forums online about puppies who've become infected with parvovirus from fox pee, and there's a litter of foxes that live at the back of my garden and lounge about the lawn as if they're on holiday in Benidorm, then scatter discarded takeaway boxes on the grass. Foxes are the litter louts of the animal kingdom.

Hardly sleep because I'm so excited about picking him up tomorrow.

23 JUNE

Mike and I pack my car with a big Quavers box foraged from Sainsbury's. I've lined the box with puppy pads, a blanket and the stuffed pig. Off we set for the farm-steading.

After two hours, we reach the farm and see Lorraine standing in the yard, holding a chubby, fluffy ten-week-old puppy. He's doubled in size since I first met him, when I could hold him in one hand, but he's still my puppy – eyes like Minstrels, world map on his back. Hello, Dennis, my tiny friend.

He doesn't like being in the Quavers box so I hold him the whole way south as Mike drives us home to Crystal Palace, where he immediately canters into the garden and does a poo on the lawn (Dennis, not Mike). Why do people complain so much about puppies? Seems house-trained to me.

24 JUNE

Wake at 5 a.m. to the pitiful sound of Dennis mewling in his crate at the end of my bed. Although the word 'wake' implies I slept. Did I sleep? Dennis cried at 10 p.m. when we put him into the crate, then I got up at around 2 a.m. and 4 a.m. to carry him blearily into the garden for a wee before stumbling back to bed. When Mike left for work, I fought the urge to say 'Stay! Help! What do I do now?'

Dennis can't go outside yet because he hasn't had his second jabs, so we sit in my kitchen all day and blink at one another in bewilderment. I offer him the stuffed pig, then the stuffed sheep, then roll a tennis ball across the floor, but he seems to tire of them all very quickly, then looks back at me as if for help, his little eyes knitted together with worry.

That afternoon, I burst into tears, overwhelmed by this sudden restriction on my life. I can't go to Sainsbury's. I can't go for a walk. I can't go out in the evening. What have I done?

I ring my friend Katie, who's just had a baby.

'It's such a big life change,' I wail.

'It is,' she agrees soothingly. 'But at least your nipples aren't raw.'

I text Mike later. 'Thank you for being the most supportive man I've ever met.' He didn't get much sleep either and I feel responsible, given that I was the one who forged ahead with this puppy thing.

'Thank you for being you,' he replies, which cheers me up a bit.

25 JUNE

I take Dennis to the vet in Gipsy Hill for injections and the receptionist asks for his registered name. 'Dennis Money-Coutts,' I say, and she bursts out laughing.

Back home, he falls asleep beside my leg as I write on the sofa, and I watch his little fat, furry tummy moving up and down for several minutes, feeling like a new mother gazing into the cot. This thought then embarrasses me. He's a puppy, Sophia, not a baby. Don't be silly.

26 JUNE

My heel rolls over what feels like a cork as I hang the washing on the clothes horse in my sitting room. It's not a cork. It's a small poo.

Mike texts me a picture of him and Dennis from the weekend, lying together on the sofa.

'Your boys,' he says.

'My boys,' I reply, with a heart emoji. (People in love are gross.)

Later, I go into my bathroom and find that Dennis has shredded every single loo roll in the basket. It's as if it's snowed inside – scraps of white tissue carpet the floor, and there's Dennis asleep in the middle of it all, legs flung out in front of him like a marathon runner who's over-exerted himself. Make a mental note to keep loo roll off the floor in the future. Quietly reach over him and remove the loo brush for good measure.

27 JUNE

I have to get out. *We* have to get out, even though Dennis can't be put down on the pavement before his jabs kick in. It's too claustrophobic staying at home all day.

I take him for a stroll around Crystal Palace, in a bag slung over my shoulder, and pass a couple with a tiny baby in a papoose. 'Snap!' I say, nodding to Dennis's fluffy head, poking over the side of the bag. The new father looks horrified.

28 JUNE

'Are you in love with your puppy?' messages my friend Eve.

Eve is my wise, no-nonsense PR friend who I met during my first job in journalism, on the *Evening Standard*. We both moved on from the paper at around the same time but stayed in touch, consoling one another over the years, usually regarding men. Then she met Jake, a handsome, blue-eyed magazine editor. They now have two sons, a house with a curved staircase in Camberwell, and a kitchen extension with herringbone floor tiles that could be photographed for a glossy interiors magazine. But no dog, and the boys are desperate for a dog, so Eve is keenly interested in my progress with Dennis.

Am I in love with him? Should I feel that overpowering sense of love that new mothers talk of when they're handed their little bundle in a blanket? I don't think I am in love with him, but does that mean there's something wrong with me? I send her a long voice note saying that – honestly – I'm feeling overwhelmed by five nights of broken sleep, by the endless mopping up of puppy wee on my kitchen floor, my bedroom floor, and my bathroom floor.

I'm not getting any writing done, I bleat, because I'm carrying him into the garden every half-hour so he doesn't wee inside, and I've also cancelled all meetings for the next couple of weeks to be with him. Dennis is making me feel claustrophobic, but then I feel guilty, because I look at his little face staring up at me, and think, 'How can I possibly resent you?'

'You just have the puppy blues,' Eve texts back authoritatively. 'I've read about it online.'

I google this and am relieved to discover that most people feel like me at the start: anxious, exhausted, worried they've made a mistake, unsure how to handle their puppy properly, trapped inside their house.

'My puppy blues with my golden retriever mostly ended when he turned 1,' says someone on Reddit. 'He was the biggest arsehole alive for his whole first year. Hang in there. It really does get better.'

I look down at Dennis, under the kitchen table, as he sniffs and then eats a daddy-longlegs. Just under a year to go, my friend.

29 JUNE

My new godson Luca's christening at a church in Mayfair. I leave Mike in charge of Dennis for the day and, when I get home, three glasses of champagne down after the reception, I find them stretched out together, dozing on a sunbed in the garden. My boys. We play backgammon in the evening sun. (Mike and I play. Dennis's backgammon isn't up to much yet.)

Maybe this isn't so hard?

30 JUNE

'You've just got to get a puppy and I have to get pregnant,' my sister Rosie said last autumn, a few weeks after Mum was diagnosed with a brain tumour. We were trying to think of things for her to look forward to: an evening at home, all her children on the sofa; a trip to the coast; a puppy; a baby.

Rosie's recently married and knows she wants to have children. She and her husband were together for six years before getting married and they've bought a house together. They seem pretty set, which I've sometimes found difficult, given that Rosie's four years younger than me and yet seems to have her life more together: husband, house, baby plans. A life unfurling with her person.

I've always been less certain about having children. I've considered the question almost every day throughout my thirties, squinting at babies in supermarket trollies while out shopping, trying to imagine if I wanted one, but I've never landed on a clear answer. Do I want them, or do I feel like I should have them because that's what everyone else does? Mike has two grown-up children, and he and I have talked about having a baby together without coming to any conclusion.

I drive Dennis to Rosie's house for dinner to prove that I've kept my end of the deal by getting a puppy, and she opens a bottle of wine and pours two large glasses, so I guess she's still working on her side of the bargain. Dennis finds a flower-pot full of dirty rainwater and cigarette butts in her garden and drinks half of it before I pull him away, panicked that he'll die overnight. Please don't die overnight, Dennis. The pet insurance doesn't kick in for another two weeks.

Rosie says he looks like Dobby, the house elf from *Harry Potter*, because his ears dwarf his little face. I tell Dennis not to listen. Soon after, he curls up and goes to sleep on my foot.

July

Things I google in July:

- my puppy just ate bit of plastic biro is that ok
- when do you fall in love with your puppy
- why is my puppy's poo so hard
- my puppy just ate two foam earplugs is that ok
- how to bath a puppy
- mole clinic south london
- can puppies eat apple cores
- my puppy just ate a match is that ok
- how to stop puppy getting into dishwasher
- 14000 steps how many calories
- getting a puppy change relationship
- bromley bin collection which day

1 JULY

I'm trying to write my weekly column for *The Telegraph* when my phone screen flashes on the kitchen table. A text from Eve: 'How are the puppy blues?'

I look around the kitchen – various stuffed animals lie on their sides on the floor as if killed in combat, a roll of loo paper is chewed and unravelled under the table, both arms of my sofa have little teeth marks in them, and chunks of discarded carrot are decorating the rug. I read frozen carrot was good for teething, but Dennis doesn't seem to like it.

He's now lying on his back, playing with an old cork he found under the radiator.

'Fine,' I reply to Eve, before googling whether puppies should play with corks, which leads me to a Mumsnet thread titled 'Can a dog choke on a prosecco cork?'

'My friend's beagle almost died from getting hold of a sweet-corn cob,' says one response.

I confiscate the cork.

2 JULY

To avoid writing this morning, I spend an hour on a dog chew website, fascinated by the animal anatomy for sale. Rabbit ears with fluff still attached are a 'natural wormer'. There are pigs' ears ('a great source of protein!'), deer antlers ('full of minerals!'), camel scalp ('low fat!') and long brown sticks that look vaguely like pepperoni and are – it turns out – made from bull penis. You can choose from skinny, standard or thick penis sticks. I put a standard bag in my basket.

After that, I get back to work. A new Netflix documentary has been released, called *The Man With 1000 Kids*. It's about a Dutch sperm donor who's fathered that many children by donating to sperm clinics across Europe, as well as privately. I write my weekly Substack newsletter on the matter, ruminating about whether I'd ever use a sperm donor.

I considered it when I froze my eggs, aged 35 and single, wondering whether I should have a baby by myself. I even spent some time on sperm-bank websites. The details you can access on them is extraordinary. Not just height and hair colour of the donor, but a recording of their voice, and a sample of their handwriting. On American sperm-bank websites, if you pay extra, you can be sent an example of their creativity – a poem or song they've written, for instance. I reckon a sperm donor singing a song might put me off a bit.

3 JULY

I'm feeling guilty about Mike, and the effect that Dennis is having on our mornings in bed. Not long after he and I started going out, we discussed when it was too early for him to wake me in the morning. 'You have to hang on until 6.30 a.m.,' I'd said firmly. Mike subsequently dubbed 6.30 a.m. the 'cuddle curfew', which is the sort of disgusting in-joke that would once have repulsed me.

Our mornings are very different now. We don't even reach the cuddle curfew because I'm already out of bed, in the garden with Dennis. No more slow, sleepy mornings, hands finding one another under the duvet.

'It's only temporary,' I promise Mike that evening in my kitchen.

'I know,' he replies, before pulling me into his chest and kissing my head.

4 JULY

Dennis and I visit the local church hall to vote in the election; I didn't know dogs were allowed inside polling stations. While I exercise my democratic right, he sniffs in the volunteers' handbags for their sandwiches, and the elderly volunteers coo over him. Later, we go to my neighbour Jamie's house for an election party. I drink too much so Mike drives us home around midnight when it looks as if Labour are on their way to victory.

The penis sticks arrive from the dog chew website. They smell appalling. Bulls need a lesson on personal hygiene.

5 JULY

I put Dennis in his crate so I can go to a Pilates class but hear him crying as I close my front door and subsequently reach the class flustered and blurt out that I've just left my puppy at home for the first time. Presumably I'll soon be one of those neurotic women who talks of their 'fur baby' and says embarrassing things in the park like 'Come to Mummy.'

I hurry from the class as soon as it's finished, panicking that Dennis will still be crying.

At home, he's asleep in his crate, little black nose tucked between his front paws.

I'm definitely too feeble to manage a baby.

6 JULY

Freedom! Dennis's vaccines have kicked in, so we can go for a walk. We visit the park where I discover that Dennis is scared of the following: other dogs, noisy children, swings, pigeons, empty cans that roll along the ground making a terrifying noise, and the wind. When he hears a bark in the distance, his ears go back and he looks up at me for help. I do feel a spark of love in my chest then.

7 JULY

I pick a couple of dingleberries from Dennis's bottom. Would you do that for someone you didn't love?

8 JULY

Dennis and I go to our first puppy school class. There are eight puppies altogether, but every time the Dobermann puppy barks, Dennis scrabbles up my arm and buries his head in my neck like a cat. We learn absolutely nothing.

I was the only person there on their own; everybody else was in a couple and I quite wished Mike was with me, but he and I usually spend Monday evenings apart because work is busy for both of us at the start of the week. From bed, I update him about the lack of success in the class.

'I miss you,' he says.

'We miss you back,' I reply.

10 JULY

'What are you doing about his anal glands?' asks a middle-aged bald man in the park this morning, before he embarks on a long lecture about the peanut-butter-flavoured treats he gives his elderly terrier, Maisie, to help her anal glands stay nice and unblocked. I can't tell if this is a chat-up line.

Dennis finds an empty Durex wrapper on the same walk and sniffs it suspiciously. This is supposed to be a nice area!

11 JULY

Mike and I discussed our policy towards Dennis in the bedroom before we got him. I've always sworn that I'd never allow my dog on the bed, and certainly never under the duvet. Mike agrees. A friend of mine lets her whippet sleep between her and her other half, under the covers, which means they only ever have sex on holiday. No, thank you.

We decide that Dennis can be in his crate in my bedroom for another couple of weeks and then he should go into the kitchen. But I cave this morning for the sake of another hour's sleep and lift him onto the bed. (Mike isn't there.)

Nearly three weeks in and I'm still taking Dennis outside once or twice in the night. Whenever I look in the mirror

I see a pale, haggard woman blinking desperately back at me, and the thought that I've made a mistake is still occurring to me two or three times a day. My life is very different, all of a sudden. The dog books warn that puppies are hard work, but should it be *this* hard?

When I picked Dennis up, I signed a contract with Lorraine agreeing that she could have first refusal on him: if I changed my mind, she would have the right to take Dennis back. But I can't do that, can I? I can't be the person who gives back their dog. Must soldier on.

Before I can stop him, Dennis eats two foam earplugs from my bedside table.

12 JULY

The earplugs emerge from his bottom. Probably won't use them again.

13 JULY

It's a gloriously sunny summer day so I take Dennis to stay at Mike's in East London. We spend most of our time at my flat because I have a proper bathroom. Mike's apartment is romantic – shelves and shelves of books, with vast, old industrial windows, and we can sit on his sofa or the roof terrace and watch people jog along the towpath opposite. But it's also an ongoing refurbishment project, and there's a challenging loo situation. Mike – temporarily – only has a 'cassette' – a plastic loo with a little tray underneath, which he has to slide out and empty elsewhere, and let's say no more about that.

This evening, we decide the sunshine warrants drinks on the terrace, so I take Dennis on his first train to Hoxton, and then we catch a bus. We arrive and head to the roof, where Dennis immediately sets about eating all the pigeon shit. That night, Mike's friend Simon also comes over for sunset drinks, and I go to bed early, leaving them sitting up together with Dennis. Much later, Mike gets into bed beside me, slides an arm across my stomach and mumbles something about Dennis being sick, but says that he's dealt with it.

Maybe I could have a baby with this wonderful man who cleans up dog sick without complaining?

14 JULY

I spy a muscular dog straining on his lead in the park. It's wearing a Hannibal Lecter-like muzzle, and its owner a hoodie with a slogan that says 'Blame the breeder, not the breed.' It's an XL bully. Makes sense. Last month, *The Spectator* website published a piece that enabled readers to put in their postcode and see how many XL bullies were registered in their area, and the highest population is in Croydon, not far from Crystal Palace.

'Dennis, Dennis, come here!' I squeak, as he starts ambling towards the killer dog.

'It's alright, she's fine!' the owner shouts, noticing my alarm.

Embarrassed by my obvious panic, I make small talk and find myself gabbling about Dennis's earplug habit.

'That's nothing,' he replies, nodding towards his XL bully, 'this one ate nine remote controls in her first five months.'

15 JULY

Our second puppy school class. Dennis manages a sit, although only when heavily bribed with his favourite snack: a little sliver of packet ham. When he does 'down' for the first time, I think my heart might burst.

17 JULY

Dennis appears at the top of the stairs, proudly holding a pair of my pants in his mouth. Somehow, he fished them out of the laundry basket. Is my dog a pervert?

19 JULY

An important weekend, because I drive Dennis to Sussex to meet Mum and Beano. Mum has never put any pressure on me regarding children, but I often feel a pang of guilt whenever she mentions one of her friend's grandchildren, and I've felt this more acutely in the past few months after her diagnosis. How much time do we have left together? Should I just get on with it and have a baby? Is Dennis the same as a grandchild?

Nearly the same, maybe. Mum grew up in a house in the Kent countryside with ponies that were allowed in the kitchen, sheep and goats in the garden, and a succession of terriers. She now lives in Sussex, in a cottage surrounded by fields, down a long dusty track, with Beano, five chickens, her bird table, and a collection of conkers trailed over her headboard and strung along windowsills to ward off spiders. (Conkers, so they say, emit a chemical that spiders don't like.) She's a proper countrywoman who speaks animal, and we had long debates about the sort of dog I should get (Westie? Dachshund? Irish terrier?) before I settled on Dennis, a parson terrier, and exactly the same kind as hers.

'Hello, sweetie,' Mum says, crouching down in her garden to welcome Dennis with open arms, and I well up.

Beano growls jealously.

21 JULY

I see anal gland man in the park and wave from a safe distance.

22 JULY

Dennis starts humping his stuffed pig toy, and I feel like a parent who's discovered porn on their teenager's phone. They grow up so fast!

23 JULY

We meet a 3-year-old girl called Trixie and her family in the woods. 'Dennis, come here!' I say, trying to stop him racing over and jumping up on her.

Trixie squats on her stubby legs and wraps her arms around his head. I worry that he might growl or accidentally nip her, but he stands patiently while she clumsily pats his ears and pokes him in the eye. Moments like this make up for all the 4 a.m. wees. And the earplugs.

24 JULY

Mike and I go to a black-tie dinner because his research project has been awarded funding from a pharmaceutical business. It's the first time I've gone out in the evening since Dennis arrived, so I've booked a dog sitter. I send her roughly thirty-seven neurotic messages in advance – *this is the code for my keybox, he's been fed, he just needs to run around the garden a bit, please don't leave his water in the crate*, and so on.

As a result, I'm late to meet Mike, but then I see him standing outside the venue, in his black tie, and my heart spins. There's my handsome, clever, good boyfriend who studies genetic disorders, here to collect a grant awarded after he made an impassioned presentation to this company. I write jokes about posh people and my hair for a living; he does a real job. I reach my hand for his, happy to be out. When we return home at midnight, Dennis is asleep in his crate, so I carry him outside to the garden, still in my dress. Mike follows me, also still in black tie, and we proudly watch Dennis unsteadily squat on the grass in the dark.

First night out and he's fine.

Maybe I won't give him back to Lorraine after all.

27 JULY

Drive to the Lake District for Eve's fortieth birthday weekend.

She's rented a big house near Kendal which has a 'no dogs' rule, so I've left Dennis with Mum and Beano. This means it's the first time Mike and I can have a lie-in since Dennis arrived.

I miss him, but it's also lovely not to worry about where he is, where he's peed inside, or whether he's eating something that's going to kill him. Does that make me a bad dog owner? Do parents sometimes feel the same relief when away from their children?

'We have a mouse killer!' Mum texts, with a picture of Dennis sitting beside a dead mouse in the field next to her cottage. It's a bit like one of those trophy-hunter pictures from safari in Zimbabwe – a large, moustachioed American sitting proudly astride a dead lion.

'No!' I text back, part proud, part horrified.

'He was dawdling behind us on the walk so I went back and found him sitting beside his little trophy,' Mum texts. 'Beano v jealous.'

When I tell everyone else at the fortieth about this, they seem weirdly uninterested.

30 JULY

Furious. Have discovered that *Crazy Rich Asians* writer Kevin Kwan has borrowed my name for his new novel. Cosima Money-Coutts, his character's called, and she's a slightly witless journalist who works for a posh magazine. I used to work for *Tatler*. This can only be me?

Over the years, I've become very used to online teasing, or sometimes active hostility, towards my name. I get it, I have the silliest name in the world, and people make all sorts of assumptions about me as a result. Sadly, I don't have a trust fund and I'm not a millionaire heiress. My family has nothing to do with the bank anymore, promise. If it did, and I *was* a millionaire heiress, I almost certainly wouldn't be writing this in my pyjamas at the kitchen table.

Kevin Kwan's character name feels creepy and weird, I write in my Substack, before sending it out. Imagine the fury if he'd done that to someone else with a 'funny' name. But because I'm considered posh, it's fair game.

31 JULY

The Mail and *The Times* have picked up on the story about my name, and the latter's stuck it on their front page with the headline 'My name's been stolen!'

No word from Kevin Kwan. Rude, I think.

Funny how many people pretend to be perfect human beings on social media these days, when their behaviour in real life suggests otherwise.

Meanwhile, Dennis gnaws on a penis stick, oblivious. 'Bad luck, because technically it's your name too,' I tell him from the kitchen table.

August

Things I google in August:

- best long lead for dog training
- games to play with puppy five months
- did victorians use chamber pots
- how to get rid of grass seeds dog's ear
- can dog get mosquito bites
- puppy keeps eating tissues
- can dogs get sunburn
- how to say beware of the dog in french
- how to say do you have a bone for my dog in spanish
- do dogs care if you fart
- how to trim dog's eyebrows
- are slugs poisonous for dogs
- prince william's beard
- bromley bin collection today

1 AUGUST

I've decided to bring Dennis on holiday to Europe later this month, so he and I go to the vet to collect his travel paperwork. Pre-Brexit, this used to be called a pet passport and was a straightforward process. Post-Brexit, it's an expensive nightmare that means waiting for forty minutes at the vet while they check his vaccination record and stamp multiple pieces of paper. The London vet reminds me that I'll need to visit a Spanish vet before returning, for them to administer a tapeworm treatment and stamp the return paperwork. What a palaver.

'That'll be £265, please,' says the receptionist when Dennis and I are (finally) cleared to go.

He could have had a seat on easyJet for less.

2 AUGUST

Before Europe, however, Dennis and I are off to Scotland with Mum, Beano and Rosie. Not long after her diagnosis, Mum said she longed to go to the coast in a campervan. 'I want to feel the wind in my hair,' she declared. So, Rosie, Mum and I have duly planned a drive to Edinburgh to see my little brother perform his sketch show at the Fringe. Since I occasionally review cars for *The Telegraph*, Volkswagen have lent me a brand-new, £80,000 state-of-the-art campervan. Three humans, one dog, one puppy and a campsite in Scotland for three nights. What could possibly go wrong?

Within half an hour of setting off, Dennis has been sick. I packed plenty of chews to keep the dogs distracted on the journey but, unfortunately, Dennis's spinach chew has come straight back up. 'We're gonna need another bag,' Rosie says from the back seat, retching herself as she tries to clear it up.

It takes ten hours and four stops to reach the campsite, where we park up in our allotted parking space. We leave Mum feeding the dogs while Rosie and I put up her Glastonbury tent in the nearby tent field. She's insisted on bringing it because she says we won't all fit in the van at night.

Unfortunately, while making my own bed in the roof of the campervan, I discover that I've packed a single mattress topper instead of a duvet. Mum's underneath me in the main cabin, with both dogs at her feet because we decided having Dennis on the rooftop bed with me was too complicated.

'Miss you,' I text Mike. 'I'd ring but Mum's underneath me!'

'Miss you too,' he replies.

'But this time in a week, nice French hotel!'

'Really looking forward to spending time together,' he taps back.

Me too, I think. It'll be warmer in France, for a start.

3 AUGUST

Nobody slept. The rooftop bed was uncomfortable, and I may now come down with hypothermia. Mum didn't sleep with two dogs at her feet. Rosie didn't sleep in her tent because a bunch of rowdy German teenagers were pitched beside her.

I send Mike a selfie of me waking up with a scarf wrapped around my head. Briefly wonder whether I should have sent a nude instead, but the angles in the campervan are all wrong. Also, Mum's having a cup of tea in the passenger seat.

I drive us all to B&M in the campervan to buy a £9.99 duvet. Later, after seeing my brother's show in Edinburgh (very funny), we return to the campsite and make curry in the van for dinner. This is a mistake because now everything smells of curry. My hair smells of curry, my rooftop bed smells of curry, my new duvet smells of curry, my toothbrush smells of curry.

No *Corrie* tonight because the campervan doesn't have a telly, so we sit inside, sheltering from the rain, and play a game of Scrabble while the windows mist up around us. Rosie puts down 'dizi' on a triple-word score, which I say isn't a word, but she claims is a type of Chinese flute. Mum comes last but says the score should account for the fact she has a brain injury.

Dennis also smells of curry, but he doesn't seem to mind.

4 AUGUST

A storm blows in, and Rosie's tent blows down at midnight, so we all squeeze into the van together. When I need a pee at 2 a.m., I clamber down from the roof into the driving rain and squat in the drenched grass because the communal bathrooms are a five-minute walk away.

Unfortunately, both dogs decide to get out at the same time, and Denis does a poo by the steps of another caravan.

'Dennis!' I hiss, through the wind and rain. 'Dennis, come here!' He ignores me and scampers about the campsite.

Eventually, I corral both damp dogs back into the campervan, and we all try to go back to sleep while the wind howls outside. What kind of psychopath enjoys camping?

5 AUGUST

Rosie returns to London because she needs to get back for work, and Mum and I motor north to Balmoral. This is another trip that Mum, a devoted royalist, wanted to make, to see the castle and its grounds. I had booked an Airbnb in advance because, prophetically, I seem to have known that we might want to sleep in proper beds by this point.

When we arrive at the Airbnb – a small, isolated lodge on the side of a hill – I almost cry with joy. A real bed! A nearby loo! I won't have to run around outside at 2 a.m. chasing Dennis!

'By the way, yesterday was ten months,' I text Mike that evening, having suddenly remembered the date through my fug of tiredness, because we're still at the point where we're counting every month like lovesick teenagers.

'Happy anniversary, darling,' he replies, with a laughing emoji.

7 AUGUST

Balmoral is surprisingly dog friendly – they're allowed to run around all over the grounds and gardens. Dennis isn't very keen on the pet cemetery, a wooded area where small headstones list the names of the late Queen's corgis, but he likes the coffee shop (scones the size of top hats). Neither dog does a poo in front of the castle. 'Out of respect,' says Mum.

Back at our Airbnb, I write my *Telegraph* column about our visit and the expensive gift shop – £70 for a tartan bow tie! I bought a bundle of organic broad beans from the King's vegetable patch for dinner instead, for the comparative bargain price of £2.

A chef friend who's cooked for the royals in Scotland says the Balmoral gardeners visit the kitchen every morning and tell the chefs what's looking best that day – green beans, beetroot, fat radishes, sticks of rhubarb and so on – and the chefs plan the day's menus accordingly. Beats trawling the aisles of Sainsbury's.

8 AUGUST

Back to Sussex in one day – 550 miles from Balmoral to Mum's house. I send Mike our live location on WhatsApp so he can follow us down and he texts me constant encouragement – 'Say hello to Shevington', 'Almost at Birmingham!' and so on. Finally, just after 5 p.m., we get back to Mum's.

The campervan still smells of curry.

9 AUGUST

Away again immediately. Mike, Dennis and I set off for Folkestone at 4 a.m. The pet reception at the Eurotunnel terminal is like Crufts: dogs of all shapes and sizes, with owners saying things like 'Sit down, Rupert, good boy.' Lots of Labradors seem to be going to the South of France for their holidays.

Paperwork stamped, we clamber back in the car and drive on to the train. Half an hour later, we're in France. This never ceases to amaze me. 'We went under the sea!' I tell Dennis, who seems unmoved.

After six hours on the road, we reach a fancy hotel in Bordeaux where we're stopping for the night. I'm nervous about Dennis peeing on the carpet, but the staff seem relaxed. When Mike and I sit outside on the terrace overlooking perfectly straight rows of vines that evening, they bring our drinks on a silver tray, with a copper bowl of water for Dennis.

Later, on a post-dinner walk in the grounds, he has a brief holiday romance with an Italian retriever.

10 AUGUST

We drive south to Provence. I make the mistake of suggesting the scenic route via the Gorges du Verdon, so this takes seven hours.

What do the French have against loo seats? Not a single loo seat in any of the service stations so far. And they call themselves a civilized nation.

11 AUGUST

We're staying in an apartment at the top of an old chateau in Provence for the weekend, in a little medieval village I've visited several times before because Eve's parents have a holiday home here. It's magical – cobbled streets, fresh croissants from the bakery every morning, splendidly grumpy French butcher, weekly market that sells olives the size of gobstoppers.

There's a neat symmetry to the timing because my new novel comes out in three days, and I wrote most of it while staying in the same village. The novel's about a London chef who unexpectedly inherits a dilapidated hotel in Provence, and I wanted the book to waft with the smells, sounds and sensations of the area: cicadas, lavender, pine forests, garlic, the heat of a French summer. Naturally, this meant an extended period staying there, so a kind friend of Eve's parents lent me her apartment in the chateau for two months in 2022, where I lived very happily, eating several croissants every morning for breakfast, and experimenting with French dishes like coq au vin and moules in the evening.

The apartment comes with a communal swimming pool, so Mike and I take Dennis for his first swim and coax him into the pool.

Fortunately, he's out by the time an elderly English couple come down for their early morning dip.

'Dogs aren't allowed in the communal areas!' the woman shrieks. 'You do realize there are children here?'

'What's Dennis going to do, *lick* them to death?' Mike mutters.

I'm gratified to see the husband, hiding under his Panama hat, looks quite embarrassed to be married to her.

After our swim, we stroll down to Eve's parents' house, where Eve, Jake and their two small sons are staying for two weeks. Harry, their eldest, mishears and thinks that Dennis is called Tennis. Everyone calls him that for the rest of the day.

12 AUGUST

I (accidentally) nearly kill Dennis. Our apartment at the top of the chateau is wonderfully romantic, with a balcony in the sitting room that overlooks the cypress trees and hills towards Nice. But when I emerge from the shower that evening, Mike looks alarmed.

'Soph,' he says, nodding towards the balcony.

Dennis is standing between the railings, his head poking through the bars, with a drop of around 100 metres beneath him to the cobbled street.

'Dennis!' I say quietly, hoping that he'll step back from the edge. 'Dennis!' But he stays in place.

I panic. If I step towards him, he might think it's a game and leap to his death. If I don't step towards him, might he see a pigeon and leap anyway?

'What do we do?' I whisper, frozen in my towel.

Mike reaches for a bowl from the cupboard and shakes it gently. 'Dennis, Dennis, what's this?'

As smoothly as Tom Cruise stepping away from a cliff, Dennis looks over his shoulder, reverses a couple of steps and trots over for a sniff of the bowl. I exhale with relief.

'You turned grey when you saw him,' Mike later remarks. Of course I did. It would have been extremely annoying to have gone to all the trouble and expense of taking Dennis on holiday only for him to jump from a top-floor balcony.

13 AUGUST

Back in the car for another seven hours to my dad and step-mother's house in Catalunya.

Dad and Shaunagh have lived in northern Spain since I was a teenager. They're nomads who prefer life away from the politics and climate of Britain, and have created a house full of treasure – ceramic Greek jugs, Turkish cushions, woven baskets from Ethiopia – collected from their travels around the world. After Dad and Mum divorced, my childhood was spent moving around, depending on where each parent was living at the time – Sussex, London, the borders of Scotland, Kent, northern Spain, back to London. But Dad and Shaunagh's part of Spain is my favourite place in the world – the longest home I've ever known.

They're away at the moment, so they've lent me and Mike (and Dennis) the house for a week. On the drive, in a traffic jam outside Montpellier, Mike and I become so desperate we play I-spy. Then we go silent for the last three hours, bored of the car and bored of bad French service-station sandwiches. I had romantic visions of this trip, but it doesn't feel very romantic as I wait for Dennis to do a poo in yet another service station, sheltering from the sun under a pine tree. Might have been easier to fly. Might have been easier to leave Dennis at home.

After the service station, we stick on a podcast about an

American cult in which women in their twenties were forced to marry a repulsive bigamist in his eighties.

So, it could be worse, I remind myself, as we crawl towards the Spanish border.

14 AUGUST

It's 36°C in Spain, and Dennis keeps panting and flopping down on the kitchen tiles.

'Is it too hot for the poor little boy?' Mum texts from Sussex, like an anxious grandmother.

'No!' I reply, because she warned me multiple times before I left that it might be too hot for him on holiday. 'He's having a lovely time!'

The mosquitoes are terrible. According to Google, dogs can get mosquito bites. Feel intense guilt for being bad dog owner who will be responsible for Dennis dying from either heat or mosquitoes.

15 AUGUST

My new novel comes out today, so we go to the nearest beach for lunch to celebrate. It's my sixth romcom, so I've learned by now that publication day is often an anticlimax. You spend months and months – years! – working on a novel, rewriting it over and over again, tightening the plot, perfecting sentences, worrying that the romantic hero isn't seductive enough, talking about it on social media, promoting it over and over again until you feel heartily sick of your own book. And then – finally – it comes out and someone on Amazon immediately says, 'ONLY GIVING THIS ONE STAR BECAUSE I COULDN'T GIVE IT NONE!!'

I bring a bone from the local butcher to distract Dennis during lunch and he spends two hours digging in the sand, flicking it all over the diners on the table behind him, burying the bone as deep as he can. Luckily, the Spanish seem to like dogs.

16 AUGUST

Mike and I canoe down the nearby river with cans of cold Estrella tucked at our feet. Dennis doesn't come canoeing because I was worried he'd fall in.

It's bliss – floating along together, laughing as we crash into the trees hanging overhead.

'Next year, we can bring him in a little life jacket,' Mike says, and my heart smiles in my chest. We talk about next year, and the year after that, and whether he'll sell his apartment and move in with me. We're making plans in a way that I never have with anyone before. I was so determinedly single before meeting him. I had a great life. I was independent, tied to nobody. But the truth is, being with someone, making plans for a life together, is very lovely. Especially after three cold beers.

19 AUGUST

Our last day. I tiptoe around the garden picking up every dog poo I can find so that Dad doesn't shout at me when he returns in a week. Mike has come down with food poisoning after eating a dodgy prawn and lies in bed all day making noises that suggest he's close to death.

20 AUGUST

Wearily, we pack up the car and get back on the road to France. Mike still isn't feeling great, although he manages to force down an almond croissant from the service station. Several hours later, we stop at another French hotel for the night, and I leave the boys in our room and recover from the drive with my book on the lawn.

An hour or so later, when I see Mike and Dennis emerge from the hotel and come towards me, I push myself up on my elbows and think, 'A year ago I didn't have either of you, and now I have both.'

It's not meant to sound smug – Mum's brain tumour has taught me how quickly things can change – but in that second, with the crickets chirruping in the background, life feels pretty special.

21 AUGUST

I wake early in the hotel and quickly take Dennis outside, leaving Mike in bed. Unfortunately, Dennis wees on the carpet in the hallway before we can get outside.

When I return to our room, Mike is quiet and the atmosphere is tense, as if he's somehow travelled away from me in the brief twenty minutes Dennis and I were gone.

'Are you OK?' I ask.

He looks at me for a few moments before replying. 'I think I'm starting to feel the effects of Dennis.'

I don't know what this means. I look at Dennis and feel guilty on Mike's behalf; I look at Dennis and feel guilty for the horrible, sudden wish that I'd never got him. He's definitely changed our relationship: no lie-ins, less going out, less sex. But these things are only temporary, I've told myself over and over again, because Dennis won't be a puppy forever. It's just for now.

'Are we breaking up?' I ask Mike, my voice cracking, suddenly panicked, sensing something strange and undefinable going on between us. A weird energy.

'Don't catastrophize,' he replies, pulling me into him for a hug. 'Why would we be breaking up?'

But we drive away from the hotel in silence and Mike decides to return home to London instead of carrying on to Devon for the weekend with my friends as planned. I try not to cry while glancing over my shoulder at Dennis, curled on the back seat, asleep, head on my flip-flop.

Was getting him a mistake?

22 AUGUST

Dennis and I continue our road trip without Mike, heading to the West Country for the bank holiday weekend. We stay with my aunt Clare for one night, on the edge of Dartmoor, and she and I sit in her garden, drinking wine while Dennis digs in her flowerbeds. 'Tell me about Mike,' she says.

He's wonderful, I tell her, he's a funny, brilliant academic, and more open and communicative than anybody I've ever been with. What I don't say is that I can't shake a sense of unease about how we left things at Folkestone Station – tearily, awkwardly – and that our messages since have been stilted.

In bed, I text him and say that I'm sad he's not with us, and also that I feel a bit rejected at having organized the holiday only for him to turn around and say he didn't want to come to Devon. He replies saying there wasn't much he could do about getting food poisoning.

At 2 a.m., I wake to Dennis scratching on the door, so let him downstairs, but he wees on my aunt's carpet before I can find the keys.

23 AUGUST

Dennis and I drive to a remote patch of Dartmoor for a walk before heading on to South Devon for the weekend. I pull up in a National Trust car park, put on his lead and walk a hundred metres or so away from the road before letting him off. It's glorious up here – a late summer day with wispy clouds scudding across the blue sky, spongy moss and heather underfoot, the excited chirp of warblers above us, plus a few watchful cows and a herd of sheep.

Too late, I remember that Dennis has never seen sheep before.

'Dennis!' I shout, as he skips towards them. 'Dennis!'

The sheep start moving as one, swarming back down the hill towards the car park as Dennis chases them.

'DENNIS!' I bellow furiously. I start running after him, shouting continually – 'Dennis! Dennis!' – but it does no good as I watch the sheep run past the car park and across the road.

I sprint after them and carry on running for another minute or so until I see the sheep stop. Where's Dennis? I can't see any flash of white among the gorse bushes and heather. Desperately, I turn back to squint at the road and car park beyond, and my heart drops into my boots. I can see a man standing there, both arms in the air, waving wildly at me. Oh my God, Dennis has been hit by a car. He must have been hit!

I run back, panting, panicking. I've had my dog for just over two months and I've already killed him. I shouldn't have got him in the first place. I am an irresponsible, useless, terrible dog own—

As I near the waving man, I see another chap standing next to him, Dennis in his arms, his tail waggling back and forth excitedly, as if he's just been on a great adventure.

'Look at me!' Dennis's expression says. 'Did you see me with those fluffy big dogs? Aren't you proud?'

I take him back as the local says, in a gruff accent, 'I'd never let my dog off a lead up here.'

'No, I know, I'm so sorry,' I stammer back, between breaths.

'I grew up in the country, so I do actually know about keeping dogs under control. Or trying to. The trouble is we don't see many sheep in Crystal Palace.'

Neither of them laugh.

I hate my dog in that moment, but I'm so relieved that he's safe I love him furiously too.

Call Mike three times that evening but he doesn't pick up.

24 AUGUST

Bank holiday weekend in Devon and the sun's out. Technically, it's glorious: a big house overlooking a valley of cows, lots of friends, scampi in the coastal pub where the tide often comes up and carries away unsuspecting tourists' cars from the car park, dairy ice-cream, Dennis racing up and down the estuary with my friend Sarah's dachshund, Sprinkles.

Except Mike's still not speaking to me, and it's making me feel panicked. I've called him another three times to no reply. What have I done?

25 AUGUST

Mike calls but he's angry. Angry at my having organized everything on holiday in France and Spain. Angry at my message about him not coming to Devon. Angry that I paid for everything, intending to sort out the bills between us later. 'I felt like a child,' he spits.

I sit on a beanbag in the playroom of the Devon house, Dennis at my feet, and feel cold.

I want to say 'What's happened? Why are you so cross with me? I organized everything on holiday because I wanted it to be perfect!'

Instead, I end up apologizing to him. What's going on? Why has he changed?

26 AUGUST

Finally back to London. Dennis immediately trots into the garden and patrols the fence perimeter, checking no squirrels have moved in since we've been away. Mike comes over in the evening and we talk. He tells me he feels like he's losing his independence because he's subsumed himself so fully into my life – hanging out with my friends, coming on holiday to my parents' house, spending more time at my flat than his.

I feel a pang of understanding because, some years ago, I read a piece by a woman who wrote about losing her sense of self in her relationship. At the time, I was with a comedian whom I loved, but I wasn't sure if I loved him quite enough, and when I read her phrase 'losing one's sense of self', it struck a chord. In eighteen months with the comedian, I'd spent so much time backstage at comedy gigs, and listening to his music and hanging out with his friends, that I'd lost sight of what I wanted. I was simply so happy to be in a relationship, so happy to feel like everyone else, that I hadn't considered whether it was the right relationship.

'But we're OK?' I check with Mike, as I stand at the oven.

He pulls me into his chest. 'We're great,' he says reassuringly.

'I'm sorry I've been a dick. I think I'd forgotten how lucky we are.'

Afterwards, we lie on the sofa watching telly, Dennis stretched out on the carpet beneath us, holding on to one another. It'll be fine, I know, because this relationship is for the long haul. This is just our first sticky moment. We've had almost a perfect year; it was bound to come along sooner or later.

28 AUGUST

Take Dennis for his first haircut at a dog spa in Beckenham.

'Pop back in an hour or so,' the nice lady at the grooming salon tells me, so I go to a nearby coffee shop and wait anxiously.

When I return, I look at him and make a strangled noise of alarm that I turn into a cough. His coat is so short it looks as if he's off to join the army.

'Lovely!' I say brightly, in the same way you'd reassure a hairdresser who'd just given you a surprise buzzcut. Dennis looks embarrassed, so I hurry him back into the car before anyone can point and snigger.

I nearly send a photo to Mike, who's taken his youngest son on holiday in Italy for a week, but then stop myself. I keep remembering the phrase he used at the end of our road trip – 'I'm starting to feel the effects of Dennis' – and I don't want him to think the only thing I can think or talk about is the dog.

I can definitely talk about other things.

Posters have gone up on lampposts along my street, with

a very unflattering picture of an enormously fat local cat, and a plea that people stop feeding him.

'Help Dash!' says the poster, before his owners go on to explain that the vet says Dash's size is taking 'a major toll' on his health: 'To help him get back to a healthy weight, we kindly ask that everyone stops feeding him, no matter how much he begs. While a small snack seems harmless, it all adds up as he visits multiple houses throughout the day.'

After so many croissants and crisps and rosé and chorizo while on holiday, I wonder if I should put a similar poster on my own fridge.

29 AUGUST

It's one of those glorious late summer days – blue skies and dazzling sunshine. Dennis ignores my pleas and digs in a big terracotta flowerpot while my sheets flap on the laundry line.

Rosie comes over for dinner, so I tell her about Mike and I having a wobble during the Devon weekend.

'But it's all good now?' she says.

'Yeah,' I reply. 'Back to normal now. All good.'

September

Things I google in September:

- puppy ate a whole sock
- dog tapeworm treatment
- how long leave dog in evening going out
- did victorians wear watches
- what age puppies most difficult
- when stop puppy crate at night
- hair locket for puppy hair
- when puppies fully grown
- is sheffield the north
- pregnant day 10 cycle possible
- how to train puppy not chase ducks
- retractable lead with shock absorber
- 11 months relationship end of honeymoon period

3 SEPTEMBER

Mike lands from Italy at midnight and comes straight to my flat, sliding into bed at 2 a.m. We fall on each other even though it's the middle of the night, as if to make up for lost time.

In May, at a party after several drinks, Mike said something which I've thought about often since: 'Let's not *not* try.'

In other words, why didn't we leave whether or not we have a baby up to fate? We wouldn't try, but we wouldn't try *not* to get pregnant, either.

I've heard friends give this advice to others before. 'Why don't you just not *not* try and see?'

But this is the same as trying to have a baby, isn't it? If you're not using contraception, and you're having sex, guess what: you may end up pregnant.

I laughed off Mike's suggestion at the party, but more recently, I've started to change my mind. We could not *not* try? I love him and we're making plans for our future. Would a baby be the worst thing?

4 SEPTEMBER

Spend most of the day in a Knightsbridge hotel suite interviewing the actor Alex Hassell, a rising star who's landed a new role in a Disney series. Seems quite reserved, but he tells me he did a naked cartwheel before a full-frontal scene to make the crew feel more relaxed, so he can't be that shy.

Afterwards, I nip to the Waitrose nearby to buy dinner. Mike's brought back pasta, wine and Parmesan from Puglia, so I want to make an authentic bolognese with chicken liver. While cooking, I give Dennis a piece of liver. He spits it out on the kitchen floor.

This is the dog who will eat brown wet wipes in the park.

6 SEPTEMBER

Off to Mum's cottage in Sussex for ten days to dog-sit Beano while she's on holiday with friends in Sardinia. There are late blackberries on the hedgerow and ripe apples on the tree in her garden. As soon as we arrive, Dennis and Beano fight over a cow's ear chew, so I put it out of reach on top of the fridge.

7 SEPTEMBER

Dennis does a poo in Mum's bedroom. I thought we'd cracked the house-training but clearly not quite. Possibly a dirty protest because I confiscated his cow's ear.

10 SEPTEMBER

Etiquette expert William Hanson has a new book out about manners which I've been sent in advance to review. It's waspish and very funny, a more contemporary, tongue-in-cheek version of the 1996 Debrett's guide to manners, which every new employee of *Tatler* was given to study when I worked there. That book was very strict about all sorts of things, including how you should eat a pear (with your left hand),

and caviar ('from the small pad of flesh between the thumb and the forefinger').

William's modern version contains guidelines on asking for someone's Wi-Fi password (don't do it the second you arrive at their house), and what to do it you see someone's flies are open. 'I was once at dinner with friends,' he writes, 'and I noticed the host's flies were undone. Now, had I made eye contact and touched my own flies, the evening could have gone in a different direction. Instead, noticing his Apple Watch, I visited the lavatory, messaged him, and by the time I had come out of the loo, the flies were fastened.'

His book is full of vital tips like this, I write in my Substack.

12 SEPTEMBER

Mike comes down to Mum's cottage. We watch TV before taking the dogs for a twilight stroll around the field. Does the sun feel more precious at this time of year as we begin to lose it, or am I just being overly romantic because Mike's with me and it feels like, after all the driving and the travelling, we can have some normal time together? That's all I want. Normality as we slide into autumn. No long road trips, no long stretches apart, back to evenings at home in Crystal Palace before falling into bed with one another.

Our one-year anniversary is approaching, so I suggest that we walk the same route we did on our first date, along the North London towpath, and end up in the same bar for a drink.

Mike gives me an 'Are you being serious?' look, and I blush.

'OK, maybe that's too cringe,' I say quickly, to cover my embarrassment.

13 SEPTEMBER

Still in Sussex. Mike and I go to my friends Matt and Grace's house in a neighbouring village for dinner. We order an Indian from the Petworth takeaway, which I often think must be the poshest Indian in Britain because during shooting season it offers pheasant tikka masala and partridge korma.

Over dinner, I hear Mike telling Grace that he's always wanted to buy a ruin in Italy, but because my dad and Shaunagh have lived in Catalunya for twenty years, and that's where my heart is, maybe we'll end up retiring in Spain. I reach for his hand under the table.

14 SEPTEMBER

Drop Mike at the local train station, and drive Dennis and Beano to the nearby deer park. Dennis has never come across deer, but they usually tend to stay down the other end of this park.

As soon as we walk in, I see a few of them eating conkers underneath a horse chestnut tree and the dogs go berserk, tangling their leads together as they strain after them. I feel like a harried mother in a supermarket – one child having a tantrum in the trolley, the other sitting in the middle of an aisle, refusing to stand up again. 'Get a grip,' I tell the dogs, who take no notice.

'I miss you,' I text Mike.

Try not to mind that he doesn't text it back.

15 SEPTEMBER

Prince Harry is 40 today. The papers are full of it: will he have a party in California? Will his brother send him a message? Will he speak to his father? Depending on what you read, he's either becoming a sad, embittered middle-aged man or living his best life in America with his young family, free from the pressures of monarchy. At moments like this, I don't miss working for newspapers and having to write such conjecture. I'm reminded of my two favourite *Daily Mail* headlines ever, both genuine and from the time that I worked for the paper in my early thirties.

1. THE DOWNSIDES OF BEATING CANCER
2. IS YOUR SHAMPOO MAKING YOU FAT?

Why is so much fuss made about turning 40? Maybe I'm feeling overly sensitive because it's my turn in a few months and for women, particularly single women without children, it's a landmark moment: the moment at which we have to start paying closer attention to our chin hairs.

People have already started badgering me – 'What are you going to do for your fortieth?' – but why do I have to do anything? I think I'd just like a quiet dinner with my family and Mike. (And Dennis. I wonder what he'll get me?)

17 SEPTEMBER

Mum gets back from Sardinia, so I drive home to Crystal Palace with Dennis and take him to the park. After bounding around the countryside for ten days, he's uncontrollable in London and chases a goose into the lake.

'Dennis, get out!' I hiss, as his head emerges from under the water, his nose covered with algae.

'It's a £60 fine if your dog goes in the lake,' says a bossy woman hovering nearby.

'He hasn't got £60 because I'm docking his pocket money for the next month,' I tell her, to which she has no reply.

We go home and I order a retractable lead on Amazon.

18 SEPTEMBER

Mike tried to break up with me this evening. He came over and started talking about our relationship as I was cooking dinner in the kitchen, saying we 'inhabit different worlds'.

'Are you ending this?' I asked, eventually grasping what he was getting at, lowering myself down next to him on the sofa. My hands were shaking.

He said he wasn't sure (OK!), so I begged for a couple of weeks to just see, to have some time together in London – normal life together. It felt such a crazy, sudden decision otherwise, when he'd talked so often of spending the rest of our lives together.

He agreed to a couple of weeks, so we went upstairs and watched yet another new police drama on TV, although I could barely concentrate on the plot because my world suddenly felt so unstable. Couldn't eat a mouthful of dinner, although Mike managed to put away three sausages.

Talking of which – an update on Dash, the fat neighbourhood cat, went up on the local lampposts today, with a picture of him sitting on a set of weighing scales. According to his owners, Dash was 5.2 kg, and he's now 4.9 kg, which means he's lost 300 g in three weeks.

His target weight is apparently 3.7 kg, so there's some way to go, but as dieticians always say, slowly does it.

19 SEPTEMBER

He did break up with me. Left. For good, I think. When we were lying alongside one another this morning, I could still feel a gap between us. Or more of a crevasse, really. Something unspoken despite everything that was said yesterday.

'How are we leaving things?' I asked quietly, staring at the light coming through the curtains, because I couldn't look at him. 'Are we going to see, or pause it, or is this it?'

Mike didn't reply for so long. It could only have been twenty seconds, but it felt like hours.

'I think this is it,' he said, eventually.

'It doesn't make sense,' I repeated again and again. Days ago, he was telling friends that he wanted to retire to Spain with me. He was suggesting we try for a baby. None of it made sense.

I cried beside him while he lay on his back, staring at the ceiling. 'I feel completely numb,' he said. 'I don't feel anything.'

So I made him get up and take his things. I couldn't lie there sobbing while he mumbled about himself.

He left not long after, as I knelt in the hallway, wailing into my hands, with Dennis standing beside me, tail moving slowly from side to side, looking up in confusion.

By mid-morning, my face was so puffy I looked like someone with a dangerous allergy who'd sniffed a peanut.

'Hope you're OK,' Mike texted.

I cannot fathom how he suddenly sounds like such a stranger. I texted back that we couldn't be in contact while I tried to process what had happened, although it wasn't what I wanted to say. 'Come back!' I wanted to say. 'Come back. I don't understand. Come back.'

You cannot smoke, your mother's recovering from a brain tumour, I told myself, as I marched to the nearest newsagent for a pack of cigarettes. But I needed one, and then another, and then another. I smoked them in the garden, as Dennis kept dropping a tennis ball at my feet, as if a consolation present.

Through red eyes, I looked at him and wondered: is it all due to you?

When Daniela the cleaner let herself in, I gestured towards my face and explained. She gave me a sympathetic look and vanished into the kitchen.

'Sophia!' she shouted moments later. 'Sophia!'

'Oh good,' I thought from my bedroom, momentarily pausing my sobs. 'Some Brazilian wisdom from an elder!'

I stuck my head through my bedroom door.

'Sophia,' she continued, 'I think it is best if you get a new vacuum.'

20 SEPTEMBER

Drive to my stepsister Elizabeth's house in Kent for the weekend, and we go to the pub, where she orders us two large
glasses of wine. I cry, yet again, as I relay everything that
Mike told me during our break-up conversation. He didn't
say much, I tell her, he didn't really explain anything. When
I finish my glass of wine, I go outside for a cigarette and am
overwhelmed by the urge to message him.

'This is unbearable,' I text. 'I'm just so sad.'

'I'm sorry too,' he replies. 'Can you send me the number of
the friend who has my coat?'

He left his coat in the Lake District when we went up
there for Eve's fortieth weekend, and one of the guests who
lives in East London, not far from his apartment, brought it
back down. Why is he worrying about his coat right now? He
sounds like a robot. Decide I won't drink any more for the
time being. Doesn't help.

Elizabeth and her husband have just spent a year doing their
house up and their spaniel, Noodle, isn't allowed upstairs, but
under the circumstances Dennis is allowed to sleep on my bed.

'No accidents on the new carpet, please,' I tell him. 'That's
all we need.'

21 SEPTEMBER

Wake early in Kent and take Dennis and Noodle for a walk.
My head is a hamster wheel, going over various moments of
our relationship again and again, so I take a photo of the
light breaking over the coast in the distance and stick it on

Instagram. 'I'm suddenly and unexpectedly a bit heartbroken,' I write, 'or very heartbroken, really. And I've been here before but would welcome anyone's wise tips.' I'm a bit embarrassed to post this. I normally make jokes on social media.

The response gets me through the rest of the weekend. So much kindness! Some send practical advice (hot baths, magnesium salts, stay off the alcohol, drink all the alcohol, eat nourishing food, eat chocolate, watch crap TV, meditate, walk, and so on), others send book suggestions, podcast suggestions and philosophical quotes. It's more comforting than I could ever have imagined. Turns out social media can be put to good use. Sometimes.

'He was BESOTTED and you're going to be SO SKINNY for your wedding,' Eve texts, when I say that I'm smoking and not eating anything. 'That's how confident I am that he'll be back.'

Elizabeth has friends over for dinner that night, but I constantly excuse myself to go outside and cry while smoking. On one of these trips to the garden, I see a small dog poo on the new hallway carpet. Dennis! I quickly reach down, pick it up with my hands and fling it in the downstairs loo.

This is what it's come to, I think, as I light my cigarette outside: crying while picking up my dog's poo with bare hands.

22 SEPTEMBER

Dennis sleeps on my bed for the first time at home. It's not quite the same as rolling over in the middle of the night and finding Mike's hand or back. Mike didn't bark whenever he heard a noise outside, either. But it's comforting, nonetheless.

23 SEPTEMBER

Fall into conversation about castration with a dog walker on our morning stroll, because Dennis is nearly six months, and some vets recommend they have the snip at this age.

'Why don't you get him chemically castrated and see how he behaves?' the dog walker asks me.

I nearly suggest that this sounds like a good idea for men who say they want to spend the rest of their lives with you before ending things two days later.

Eve sends me a break-up care package with a box of camomile teabags and chocolate. My friend Clare has sent me magnesium bath salts and a book of ghost stories by a Victorian writer called M. R. James. 'Because it's my theory that you cannot be both heartbroken and terrified at the same time,' she writes in the card. My friend Hannah sends me a stern message saying I need to take melatonin so I can sleep properly.

Not for the first time in my life, I wish I was a lesbian.

24 SEPTEMBER

Download Hinge. After my last break-up, I didn't date anyone for over a year. But I'm so at sea and feel so rejected that I need the confidence hit. There are other people out there; it'll be OK. At some point, it'll be OK.

I scroll back through my photos, trying to avoid any taken of Mike weeks earlier on holiday, to find a few nice shots of me, then write several bad answers to the prompt questions and upload my new dating profile. Back on a dating app four months before I turn 40.

Meet a bulldog called Moonshine in the park that afternoon, so enormous he can barely walk. His owner tells me that he tried to suckle a cow in a field over the weekend (Moonshine, not the owner). People always say that getting a dog is a good idea if you want to meet someone, but the pickings feel quite slim in Crystal Palace Park.

Eve sends me one of her rambling voice notes asking for an update on my heartbreak diet: 'During my last break-up, someone called me gaunt, and it was the greatest compliment I've ever received.'

25 SEPTEMBER

Like some sort of deranged sociopath, I remembered my doorbell camera today and watched back the footage of Mike leaving my flat last week. It's awful; he looks through the door at me one last time, drops his head and turns in the drive, then slowly trudges away and out of sight. Meanwhile, a whale sounds like it's dying in the background.

It's not a whale – it's me sobbing.

Eve once uploaded a video from her doorbell cam to YouTube in the hope that it would go viral and pay for her kitchen extension. It was of a man wearing a balaclava, thumping their front door and demanding to be let in. Jake asked what he wanted through the door, warning him that his kids were inside, and after a brief, terse exchange, it turned out the man in the balaclava was a swinger who'd got the wrong address. At that point, Jake laughed, opened the door, fist-bumped the swinger in the balaclava, and merrily directed him to the neighbouring house. All this at 3.30 p.m. on a weekday afternoon.

Go to an important work dinner this evening with the producers who've bought my fourth novel. Mustn't bang on about the break-up, I tell myself, as I walk towards the Italian restaurant.

When I reach it, I see them sitting at an outside table. 'I can smoke!' I say, as I greet them both and sit down. 'Sorry, I know it's revolting, but Mike broke up with me last week.'

When I get home, Dennis is so excited to see me that his bottom waggles from side to side and his tail goes crazy. I kneel on my kitchen floor as he jumps all over me in excitement, and I burst into tears. Again.

26 SEPTEMBER

Open Hinge this afternoon as a distraction from a boring piece I'm writing about the history of the sandwich.

'I go crazy for feet!!' says the first profile I see.

I close Hinge.

27 SEPTEMBER

Did you know it's squirrel season? According to a dog walker in the park this morning, we're right in the middle of it. I later look this up online and discover he's right. The squirrel marketing board hasn't made it up; at this time of year, their numbers surge across the UK.

'One of my favourite pastimes is shooting squirrels,' says Ray732, in a forum I discover on the subject.

'I had twenty-nine from my garden last year, but I'm only on fifteen this year so far,' replies another.

'Does anyone eat them? I have heard they taste quite good but are a devil to skin,' says BryanDC.

Imagine how hungry you'd need to be to eat a squirrel.

Dennis is doing his best. He spots a twitching, fluffy tail in the park and dives after it. Then another, and another. He never catches them, and he hasn't worked out that they can run up trees, either. To him, squirrels simply vanish into thin air and he's left there, in the park, looking left and right around him in bewilderment. It makes me laugh every time.

It's one of the lovely things about having a dog, I'm realizing. They're never worrying about yesterday or tomorrow. They're very present. Dennis doesn't trudge around the park thinking about castrating his ex-boyfriend or how much he misses him. He hurries around the park thinking 'SQUIRREL! OOOH LOOK, A FRIEND WITH A BALL! QUICK WEE ON THIS PAPER BAG! THIS LOOKS LIKE A GOOD STICK! CAN I HAVE A SNACK? ANOTHER SQUIRREL!' Dogs have mastered mindfulness without having to sit through hours of boring old meditation.

Be more Dennis, I think, as we walk home that evening.

28 SEPTEMBER

I meet a friend in Battersea Park for a walk and update her about my love life as we stand in the playground, watching her kids play pirates.

'I think it sounds like he was quite complicated,' Iz says gently, and slowly I nod my head. Although I often protest whenever someone is labelled complicated, because don't we all have our complications?

I look around the playground at all the other 30-something couples – pushing buggies, chasing small toddlers – and feel myself becoming defensive all over again. Maybe I don't want this. Maybe children and Battersea Park playgrounds just aren't meant for me. Maybe I'm just going to have this one small fluffy child, who's busy chasing squirrels up trees. At least I (rarely) have to wipe his bottom.

29 SEPTEMBER

I wake up early and lie in bed scrolling on my phone. Then I open Hinge, and the very first profile I see is Mike's.

One of his pictures was taken in New York not long after we started going out. I know this because he sent it to me. I know I've downloaded Hinge again too, but I didn't want to. I don't want to be back on a dating app. I want to be with the man who left me notes saying he loved me under my pillow, and texted me sweet things throughout the day, and helped me get through my mum's illness, and drove us to collect Dennis. The man who talked about forever.

'Ouch, I've just seen you on Hinge,' I message him. 'I feel

like I'm going mad. Am I going mad? Did I make everything up?'

He replies an hour later. 'No, you didn't make everything up.'

It's oddly comforting. He did love me, it was real. Something strange has happened in the past few weeks to change that. I just wish I knew what it was.

Later, Rosie and Olly come over for a Thai takeaway and we watch the football. Dennis looks longingly at the bag of prawn crackers, so I give him one, and then another, and then another.

He's going to get very spoiled at this rate, like a child in the middle of a divorce.

October

Things I google in October:

- is it true male dumpers come back
- how long prince william and kate middleton broken up for
- dog blister on paw
- did ex break up with me because of dog
- stop dog barking in garden
- how many men regret breaking up
- why were fish knives invented
- ex picked up belongings feel even worse
- best heartbreak podcast
- dog anal glands
- when to get dog castrated
- michael barrymore tiktok

1 OCTOBER

I find Mike's wellington boots in the hallway, partially hidden by the shoe basket, and dump them in the bins outside. That's the kind of mood I'm in today.

2 OCTOBER

Discover Mike's black tie in my wardrobe, hanging between my shirts. Shit. I can hardly put that in the bin with the boots. I'm reluctant to break our silence but text him anyway: 'Found your black tie in my cupboard. Will probably burn it.'

'OK. Thanks,' is his succinct reply.

I go through the pockets like a suspicious wife but find only Rizla papers and an invitation for the charity party we went to in the summer.

My friends Lucy and Jen come for supper with their husbands, and we have a chicken pie I've made from scratch following a recipe in Julius Roberts's cookbook. Dom says it's the best chicken pie he's ever had. I do sometimes think it's weird that nobody's married me.

3 OCTOBER

Lean into the big wheelie bin and fish out Mike's boots, hoping the neighbours aren't watching. If he's got to come and collect his black tie, then he might as well have the boots back. Have brief sniff and they definitely smell of bin juice.

In the evening, I have dinner with three girlfriends at a restaurant in Bayswater where they all ask if I'm eating properly because I look thin. Never been called thin before. Thrilled.

Get home and let Dennis into the garden, then spend twenty minutes hissing his name and waving a bag of treats in the air – in my slippers and dressing gown – because he's smelled a fox and doesn't want to come inside.

How often is it normal to want to murder your dog?

4 OCTOBER

Doorbell goes. Enormous box of birdseed has been delivered. Certain journalists I know are sent free shoes and handbags, and given free Botox. I have been sent free birdseed. To be fair, it's the equivalent of Fortnum & Mason birdseed, sent to me by a nice farmer called Tom after I complained online that the birds of Crystal Palace didn't appear to like my sunflower seeds. Tom makes very posh birdseed, containing all sorts of seeds supposedly irresistible to small birds including robins and wrens, and has sent me a bag to try. I tip it into the feeder on my kitchen window and wait.

It doesn't take long for a robin to appear, darting quickly back and forth between the nearby tree and the feeder, as if he doesn't quite believe his luck and this new bounty might vanish again at any second.

Being interested in birds must be sign of age, like that weird noise I now make whenever I sit down.

5 OCTOBER

'Why don't you and Dennis come for lunch?' says my step-brother.

Great, I've become the spinster aunt whose plus one is a dog.

Harry is a wonderfully generous and cheerful man who works in finance and has a large house in Brixton with a very bulging wine fridge. We arrive and he immediately pours me a large glass of something that tastes expensive while my plus one plays in his toddler's ball pool.

Marlit, his wife, is pregnant again, which is very lovely news, obviously, but on the way home, I feel that horrible, childish sensation of being left behind. Three siblings married, with multiple children between them, meanwhile I have a dog who spent the return journey to Crystal Palace retching on a piece of plastic ball that he'd swallowed.

Got home and lay on the sofa to scroll through Hinge with renewed purpose.

'Hello again …' pops up a message from a TV producer.

Suffer momentary panic that I've now dated every man in London and they're coming back around again.

'I'm so sorry,' I reply, cringing as I type, 'but have we met before?'

Turns out we haven't. We matched years ago (did we?) but never met up. Make a date at a pub in Herne Hill for next week. Have scheduled smear tests with more enthusiasm.

7 OCTOBER

Unfortunately, the posh birdseed has created a dramatic new ecosystem in my garden. Small birds fly to the feeder and swallow the seeds but are such enthusiastic and messy eaters that they scatter some to the paving stones beneath. Pigeons, observing this carelessness from the oak tree at the end of my garden, swoop in for the droppings on the floor. Next-door's cat, spying the pigeons, pounces on them from his spot on the fence.

Dennis, watching all this from inside, goes berserk.

I try not to be too distracted by the *Jurassic Park* scenes going on in the garden while writing my Substack post. How will I be able to date with a dog, is this week's big question. When I meet the TV producer in the pub, will I be anxiously watching the clock, worrying that I need to go home and let Dennis into the garden? And having a dog doesn't allow for much spontaneity when it comes to dating. Say the TV producer and I get on famously, I can hardly go back to his for a night of passion and forget about Dennis. Nor could he come back to mine, because Dennis and I get up at 6 a.m. every morning for the first squirrel hunt of the day in the park.

None of these things are likely. I'm not sure I'll even shave my legs for this date. But I haven't ever dated with a dog before and I don't know how to do it.

8 OCTOBER

Dennis and I see Dash, the local cat on a diet, on our morning walk. He's still enormous.

Have dinner with a gaggle of old *Tatler* colleagues. 'You couldn't possibly have married a man called Mike,' declares my friend Sophie, a stylist who's always dressed in vintage Chanel.

9 OCTOBER

Dennis is six months old and celebrates by triumphantly carrying a pair of small boy's Y-fronts around the entire park in his mouth. He found them near the dinosaurs and refuses to let me take them off him. Definitely a pervert.

10 OCTOBER

Off to Liverpool to interview the author Sophie Kinsella on stage at Waterstones. In 2022, Sophie was diagnosed with a brain tumour, but has since had an operation, been through months of rehabilitation, and has somehow managed to write a novel at the same time. It's an autobiographical novel, starring a heroine who's similarly diagnosed with a brain tumour. I've been asked to do this event by Sophie's publishing team because I've interviewed her before, and also because of Mum's diagnosis and the hope that I can approach this subject with sensitivity.

In Liverpool, hundreds of people are waiting to see Sophie. She looks fabulous, in a silver dress, all smiles.

Her agent asks me beforehand if I could say something at the start to ensure there aren't any personal questions about her tumour and the prognosis.

Absolutely, I reply.

We go on stage, I make a brief introduction and ask that people keep their remarks to Sophie's books. After half an hour of talking, I open the floor to questions.

'Can I ask, what symptoms did you have?' a woman towards the back shouts loudly, despite my warning at the beginning. I wince, but Sophie calmly answers it.

The next question is from a woman in the front row. 'The Princess of Wales has talked of telling her children about her cancer diagnosis. How did you manage this?' she asks.

What is *wrong* with people?

12 OCTOBER

Dennis and I are in Dorset staying in a big house two friends have rented for the weekend to throw a joint fortieth birthday party.

We sneak out early, while everyone else is still asleep, for a drizzly walk on the nearby beach. Dennis has trouble doing his business and, on closer inspection, it turns out this was because he'd eaten a tampon and it was stuck. He must have gone into one of the bathrooms at the house and eaten one from a bin.

I crouch in the rain, on this (fortunately) deserted beach, holding my petrol station coffee with one hand while pulling the tampon string from his bottom in the other. 'Your life is so glamorous,' people used to say to me when I worked at *Tatler*.

Eventually the tampon comes free and Dennis bounds merrily up the beach, as we all might after such an event.

13 OCTOBER

Hungover and tired after the birthday party, I drive back to London. Just before Dennis and I get home, Mike sends a message saying that he's been to my flat and collected his last few bits and pieces.

I let myself in and double over in my bedroom, looking at the empty space where I'd left his black tie and wellington boots out. It feels very final.

In the past few weeks, various people have told me that break-ups are a form of grief and I've protested, because it's not as if he's died. But the black hollowness I feel in my stomach now definitely feels like grief. The absence of him. The idea that he's never coming back. I sit on my bedroom carpet and cry while Dennis patiently sits beside me.

14 OCTOBER

Rosie gives me a stern talking-to about letting Dennis sleep on my bed. 'If you ever want to have sex again, he can't stay in there.' Right now, the thought of sleeping with anyone else is unfathomable, but she's probably right. I should move him.

Also, Dennis is a restless sleeper – he sniffs, he wakes at 3 a.m. and starts licking his paws, he stretches, he squeaks as he dreams, and barks when he hears a fox outside.

I set up his crate in the spare room and put him in with a handful of kibble after his last wee in the garden. It feels like shutting the Little Princess in her attic room.

15 OCTOBER

I slept; Dennis seemed perfectly happy when I let him out of his crate in the morning. Rosie was right; this is probably for the best when I feel up to having sex with someone again in roughly five to ten years' time.

16 OCTOBER

Mike sent me a furious message today because I mentioned our break-up in my *Telegraph* column on the weekend.

Having watched a hit new Netflix series about a rabbi falling in love with a gentile, I wrote a column questioning whether different backgrounds matter these days, when it comes to dating: 'I watched it with particular interest because my ex-boyfriend recently cited my "world" as the reason he was breaking up with me,' I wrote. '"We inhabit different worlds," he said, in our final, sad conversation. He didn't like that I wrote about "posh" matters; I tried to remonstrate that it's all tongue-in-cheek and, also, I live in a maisonette in Crystal Palace, hardly a stately home, but no dice. He'd decided we were too different.'

I don't believe I said anything unkind, but he's clearly mad with anger. His long, venomous message says that my writing was vulgar and made him wince, and that I wasn't attractive enough for him.

I sit on my bed, reading the message over and over, feeling winded that a man I loved so much could possibly say these things. Then I forward it on to Rosie and Eve.

'Do not reply,' Rosie says, calling me immediately.

Eve sends me an incredulous four-minute voice note. 'I am ASTONISHED. My jaw is HANGING OPEN. I literally cannot fathom how he sat, probably on the floor of his horrible flat without a bathroom, and wrote that message, and at no point did it occur to him that maybe he should think twice before hitting send,' she shouts into her phone. 'I can't believe I said you were going to be skinny for your wedding. You're gonna be skinny for your wedding to SOMEONE ELSE!'

Women, I think, for the zillionth time in a few weeks, are the best.

Unfortunately, a few hours later, it's my date with the TV producer. Sit on the bus to Herne Hill feeling less romantic than Anne Boleyn on the way to her beheading.

Luckily, he's a vaper, so we sit outside a pub in Herne Hill, both smoking and making polite conversation about TV shows we've recently watched. I'm a child on her first day at school, unsure how to behave, unsure when I can leave.

We say goodbye after a couple of drinks and make vague promises about having another drink at some stage, but I think we both know we won't.

17 OCTOBER

Dennis and I meet a chocolate Labrador also called Dennis in the park.

This causes some confusion when his owner and I try to get our respective dogs to follow us, both shouting 'Dennis!' at them.

18 OCTOBER

'Does Dennis have a coat?' texts Megan, a local dog walker. I've booked her to come over and take him out for a walk because I've got a meeting in Soho.

No, he doesn't, I reply. Should he?

It's been endless rain in the past few days and I've noticed more and more dogs in the park wearing coats: labradoodles in fleecy coats; an elderly Westie walking stiffly along in a green coat; a dachshund in a raincoat with a translucent hood that covered its head. Poor thing looked embarrassed.

Do dogs need coats? Dennis's fluffy fur seems waterproof to me. I think it's a slightly precious city thing. You'd never catch a dog in the countryside wearing a coat.

19 OCTOBER

I've agreed to another Hinge date. After Mike's message about me not being attractive, I feel like I need to make more of an effort. There must be someone out there who thinks otherwise. Even Hitler had a love life.

This time it's with a theatre director who's suggested a coffee at 11 a.m. in Soho. It feels very American, a coffee date, when first dates for Brits usually involve eighty-three drinks and a drunken lunge at the end.

Because of all the smoking, I've come down with a terrible cough and hack through our two coffees sounding like a Victorian consumptive. This doesn't seem to put off the talkative theatre director because he texts me afterwards saying he'd like a second date. I'm not sure. He's quite short.

20 OCTOBER

The theatre director messages me, asking when we'll see each other again.

21 OCTOBER

I reply to the director, politely saying I'm going to America shortly, a trip I booked months earlier to visit a friend, so we might have to postpone our second date until after that.

He'll have forgotten about it by the time I get back. Hopefully. Should I really be dating, or forcing myself to date, when I feel this bleak about it? Maybe it's unfair. Maybe I'm being just as bad as all the ghosters out there.

22 OCTOBER

Dinner with Eve and our playboy friend Jez in Soho. Jez says I'm so thin I must be on Ozempic. You don't need Ozempic to lose weight, I tell him, you just need a very sudden break-up.

I nip outside for a cigarette during dinner and fall into conversation with a homeless Liverpudlian.

'How can you tell a Scouser's having an orgasm?' he asks.

'Don't know,' I reply.

'She drops her chips,' he replies, with a wheezy laugh.

'What d'you call a Scouser in a white tracksuit?' he goes on.

'Not sure,' I tell him.

'The bride,' he offers, with another laugh that sounds like a knackered accordion, before asking for one of my cigarettes.

I hold out my packet, then walk back inside and repeat the jokes at the table. My Scouse accent needs work.

24 OCTOBER

Spend my morning making egg mayo sandwiches in the café at the Royal Marsden Hospital, where I occasionally volunteer. Dennis, meanwhile, has gone for his first ever session at a Crystal Palace daycare centre. It's called Noah's Bark and just like a posh nursery – big leafy garden, slides, trampolines, dog toys, a sandpit for digging and a doggy paddling pool. It would be easier to get your dog into Eton, I've thought before, but luckily today they had a spare spot.

A weary-looking woman appeared in the café and asked for a coffee just after midday, before explaining that her husband was downstairs having treatment.

She stood patiently behind the counter while I tried to get the bastard coffee machine to work. It never does.

'I'm so sorry, it's being particularly slow and dribbly today,' I told her.

'If it's slow and dribbly,' she replied, with a very faint smile, 'it *could* be prostate.'

People who can laugh at black moments are my heroes.

Dennis comes back from daycare and immediately falls asleep on the kitchen sofa, exactly like an exhausted toddler.

25 OCTOBER

'UPDATE?' texts Eve.

'Alright, actually,' I text back. 'I think maybe his message was quite liberating, in a way. Because I've realized he's so different to the man I fell in love with??'

'I think his pathetic behaviour is giving you permission to release yourself from the grief,' she replies.

Eve has had a lot of therapy.

26 OCTOBER

Interview the comedian and actress Helen Lederer about her new memoir for the literary festival in Mum's local town. I've spoken here a few times, although I embarrassed myself once by reading out a specific passage from my second novel in which the heroine pees on her fingers while doing a pregnancy test. It didn't go down very well among the genteel mid-afternoon audience.

'How are you?' Helen asks, before we go on, in the chaplain's room at the back of the church where the talk is being held. I update her about my love life since we've met a couple of times before, and Helen's one of those warm people you can tell anything to. She makes sympathetic noises and we go on stage.

'Hello everyone, it's lovely to be here,' she says into her microphone, as hundreds of people look up at us expectantly. 'Now, Sophia's going through a break-up so we need to be especially nice to her.'

At least this breaks the ice.

29 OCTOBER

Mum suddenly felt faint in Tesco today, and had to sit down while I put everything through the till. 'Let's go home and have a cup of tea,' I suggested, not knowing what else to say. I've googled the statistics of her type of tumour. I think we probably all have, but we don't talk about it. Throughout eleven years of cancer, Mum has stoically carried on, never letting herself believe the worst. Or at least, never openly showing fear to any of her four children. But there are moments, like now in the car, when I think 'What if?' What if it's back?

At home I put the kettle on, and we open a packet of shortbread, after which she seems much better.

'Maybe just low blood-sugar levels?' she says, and I nod. Definitely. Let's say it was that.

30 OCTOBER

Leave Dennis at Mum's and drive to Gatwick for my flight to America. Two days in Miami followed by a week in Palm Beach, staying with my old university friend, Emily.

'Take a trip,' everyone says, after a break-up. I booked this months ago because I wanted to be in the States for the presidential election, but I feel guilty at leaving both Mum and Dennis. It'll be the longest spell I've ever been away from him. 'We'll be fine,' she insisted, waving me off down her drive.

On board, I wait expectantly for the trolley so I can have a large glass of wine with my lunch. Eventually, it trundles along and I discover with horror that British Airways no longer hands out little bottles of wine. Sometimes, if you were lucky, they even handed out two little bottles.

Instead, the air steward pours me half a plastic tumbler of Sauvignon Blanc, which I've almost finished before she moves back a row.

'Could I possibly have another glass of wi—' I begin to say, just as she snaps the trolley back.

Standards have slipped on British Airways.

November

Things I google in November:

- average time men regret break up
- how to tell off puppy when he won't come inside
- why is heartbreak so up and down
- gerry adams
- meditation for heartbreak
- dog signs blocked stomach
- gipsy hill vet emergency number
- car seat belt for dog
- how many kardashian sisters are there
- why do dogs hump
- ex-boyfriend on date feel sick
- puppy dragging bottom
- how tall is gary barlow
- bromley council new compost bin

1 NOVEMBER

I wake early in Miami, jet-lagged, and walk to Starbucks for a coffee. The card reader asks for a tip, so I add on a dollar because American tipping culture terrifies me. Would the barista spit in my coffee if I didn't tip? I carry my $8 Americano to the beach and notice various people gathering and staring at the clouds on the horizon, so I sit in the sand and watch kite-surfers whizz back and forth across the inky water. Then I realize what they're waiting for: sunrise.

The sun appears on the horizon like an egg yolk and, as I sit there, I well up. I'm so happy to be away, thousands of miles from home, that I don't even mind that I've just spent $8 on a tepid, tasteless coffee.

2 NOVEMBER

Drive from Miami to Palm Beach to stay with my old university friend. Emily is British, but her father's family were Cubans who moved to Florida after Castro took over in 1959. Emily spent holidays at her grandparents' house in Palm Beach, and now she's moved here from London with her husband, Frase, and their small son, Luca, and Mowgli the golden retriever.

I arrive and Emily immediately takes me on a tour, driving past Mar-a-Lago, Trump's house, where big black SUVs are parked outside. You can tell they're Secret Service because they say 'Secret Service' on them.

Mum sends a picture of Dennis, his front legs on the kitchen table, his nose in her cup of tea. Beano is always allowed to finish her last inch of tea, so I guess this is a habit Dennis may pick up while staying there too. I feel like one of those parents who sends the kids to stay with Granny, only for the kids to return spoiled, demanding sweets for breakfast.

3 NOVEMBER

Palm Beach has the highest population of billionaires in America, a friend of Emily's called Alan tells me proudly over dinner that night. We're in the new Nobu that's opened here, in a hotel owned by the world's second-richest man, the tech tycoon Larry Ellison. I say 'the new Nobu'. It's actually just part of the hotel lobby that's been cordoned off with a velvet rope. It was the hotel coffee shop before, but now they've put up the velvet rope, a Nobu sign on the wall, and they're serving black cod fillets for $52, so everyone in Palm Beach is desperate for a table. This place is bonkers.

Alan has already told me that he sold his last business for $350 million. Then we discuss Christmas plans. Alan and his family are going to Oman. 'Ooof,' I reply, 'that's a long journey from here.' Alan grins; 'Not in the G5.' This confuses me until he explains that a G5 is a Gulfstream. Decide not to mention British Airways' new wine policy. Don't think Alan would like it.

When I mention I'm single, Alan decides he's going to set me up with his rich friend.

I've had two lychee martinis and am fuzzy enough to think this is a fun idea. Why not go on a date with an American millionaire? You never know, he could be charming.

Alan takes a photo of me and sends it to his friend.

His reply pings back less than ninety seconds later. 'Cute but not my type.'

Ah, OK. So not *that* charming.

4 NOVEMBER

'How are you feeling?' Emily asks, as we go for a morning walk along the beach. Quite a slow walk because she's pregnant with her second baby.

'Good. Think the jet lag's worn off,' I reply easily.

'No. How are you really feeling?' she repeats.

'Oh,' I say, understanding. I'd updated her on the Mike drama on my first evening here, but the lovely thing about old friends, or one of the lovely things, is that you can return to the same topics of conversation again and again, unpicking them from different angles.

Honestly, pretty good, I tell her. Being away has helped. Discovering that he's not the person I thought he was has helped. Maybe the break-up was a good thing, long term. Also, I venture, voicing aloud a thought I've had a few times but haven't said openly, without Mike, I'd never have got Dennis. 'So that's a plus.'

'D'you love him?' (She means Dennis.)

I do, I say. I miss him. I'm surprised by how much I miss him. I miss him like a person.

'Next time, bring him,' Emily says. Apparently certain airlines would let Dennis into the cabin. She and Frase have researched this because they want to bring Mowgli back to the UK in the summer.

I tell her I can't think of anything worse than a ten-hour flight in economy with Dennis at my feet. Also, he'd hate it.

We leave the beach and walk towards Worth Avenue, the glitzy street in Palm Beach lined with palm trees and shops, including Gucci, Loro Piana and Ferragamo.

I spot a man walking a large black-and-white pig on a lead, just like a dog. 'That's Mona Lisa,' Emily says matter-of-factly. One of the town's millionaires has a pet pig called Mona Lisa, she explains, and its walker takes her up and down Worth Avenue every day.

5 NOVEMBER

Election day. *The Telegraph* wants my less political take on all the madness from Trump's Florida hometown, so I'm up early.

I catch an Uber from Emily's house to a diner near the recreation centre where Trump and Melania are going to vote. The diner is already full of Palm Beach residents fresh off the golf course – tanned, elderly men in Pringle jerseys and baseball hats. 'The future of democracy is at risk!' thunders one, as he accepts a plate of eggs from the waitress.

I order my own plate of eggs and eavesdrop on two men nearby who look like they work for the FBI and seem to think Trump's cavalcade will arrive in an hour.

Outside the recreation centre, it's mostly MAGA supporters, in MAGA hats and MAGA T-shirts. There's also a Yorkshire terrier in a MAGA jacket.

I bump into a fellow *Telegraph* journalist, and we stand on the wall at the back of the press scrum and wait for Trump to appear. 'Who's going to win?' I ask, since the polls are still saying it's too close to call.

'She will,' he says confidently, 'by a country mile.'

Secret Service men with Lego haircuts keep coming in and out of the front door, but eventually – after three hours of waiting in the Floridian sunshine – word filters out that Trump's come and gone from the back entrance. The risk of snipers was too high for him to come and wave at us.

I race back to the diner for a club sandwich and write 1,000 words about standing on a wall for three hours and still not seeing Trump.

That evening, I take out a bottle of Californian Chardonnay from Emily's fridge, and we settle on the sofa, eating pizza and flicking between the rolling election coverage on CNN and Fox News.

Frase and I debate going to the convention centre, a few miles away, where Trump will make his victory speech if he wins. Nah, we decide in the end. We're both too tired. And he's probably not going to do it. I go to bed when the result is still unclear.

6 NOVEMBER

Wake at 2.30 a.m. Check phone. Trump's won. Should have gone to the convention centre. Probably a good thing I'm not a political journalist.

7 NOVEMBER

Land at Heathrow just after 7 a.m. and drive straight to Mum's, as excited about being reunited with Dennis as I would be with a lover. I kneel on her kitchen floor and he jumps all over me, his tail waving back and forth like a windscreen wiper.

Actually, this is better than being reunited with a lover.

'By the way, he was sick this morning,' Mum declares, just after I let him lick my face. She isn't sure why, and when he's sick again, we decide I should take him to the local vet.

'He seems alright to me,' says the vet, before giving Dennis an anti-sickness injection and charging £75.

After spending a week in the town that boasts the highest population of billionaires in America, this feels quite grounding.

8 NOVEMBER

Drive Mum to Portsmouth Hospital for a routine brain MRI. We're quiet on the way there, but she's in and out quickly, and we both have a glass of wine when we get home. She'll hear the results in a few days, but we've become quite used to this waiting game in the past year or so.

9 NOVEMBER

Back to London, where I drop my bags and take Dennis to Dulwich Woods to meet Eve and the boys. She holds out a paper bag full of pains-au-chocolat, so I take one and we walk while the boys and Dennis run ahead of us.

Unfortunately, they then run back and announce they've lost 'Tennis', which means half of us are walking through the woods shouting 'Dennis!' and half are shouting 'Tennis!'

'Is he Dennis or Tennis?' asks a nearby walker, when we finally find him.

'Dennis,' I reply, as I put on his lead.

'Oh,' he says, sounding disappointed. 'Tennis is a great name.'

The theatre director texts: 'Are you back?'

Ah, so he hasn't forgotten.

10 NOVEMBER

I send a voice note to the director, saying I have tickets to a stand-up gig the following week, asking if he'd like to come. I'd bought them months earlier for me and Mike, so I might as well use them on a date, even if I'm not that sure about him.

The director replies saying that he's free, although there's an Arsenal game on, but he'll sacrifice that to see me.

This doesn't feel like the path to true love.

11 NOVEMBER

My friend Hannah texts me saying that Mike is going on a date with a friend of hers.

Hannah knows this because her friend messaged a WhatsApp group with a screenshot of Mike's Hinge profile, asking if anyone else was dating him. This is how small the dating pool in London has become: we have to check with people before a date in case anyone else is also seeing them.

Urgh. Having come back from America feeling less raw about Mike, the news about this date scrambles my brain and I spend roughly three hours stalking Hannah's friend online to see if she's prettier/thinner/cooler than me.

I update Eve on the situation. 'He is a Peter Pan man-child who overcommitted, started talking about kids with you, freaked himself out, broke your heart and is now frantically dating anyone else with a pulse to try to remind himself he's not broken,' she texts back. 'It doesn't take Freud to see this guy is on the cusp of a gap year.'

13 NOVEMBER

An editor from *You* magazine emails asking if I can go to New York next week to interview Brooke Shields because she has a new book coming out about ageing. I know almost nothing about Brooke Shields, although I vaguely remember watching her in a terrible Christmas film set in a Scottish castle on Netflix a couple of years ago. Still, forty-eight hours in New York is impossible to turn down.

'Yes please,' I reply, leaping at the chance to escape back to America so quickly. Brief pang of guilt at the idea of leaving Dennis again, but I'll find him a nice dog sitter and buy him a present.

14 NOVEMBER

Go for a drink in a Borough wine bar with an American actor, who asked me out via a DM on Instagram.

I looked him up beforehand to check that I wouldn't be murdered but, apart from the fact that he plays the violin, he appeared relatively sane.

He's charming company and has good teeth, but he's also one of those Americans who's obsessed with all things English. He can only talk about spaniels, tea, castles, crumpets and the Cotswolds. I can't marry someone like that.

15 NOVEMBER

Dennis's seatbelt arrives from Amazon. I've been meaning to get one for ages because Mum keeps saying the police will hand me a £5,000 fine if they spot him roaming around loose. Dennis treats my car much like a small child in a soft play area – constantly leaping from the front to the back and the front again depending on whether he wants to sleep or keep an eye out for cats crossing the road.

I put the harness on and clip him into the front seat. He looks very put out by this.

Watch a documentary about Brooke Shields. What a wild life. Her mother let her pose nude for *Playboy* aged 10, and her first kiss was in a film, aged 11, with a 29-year-old actor. When she was making a film aged 15, the director twisted Brooke's big toe during a sex scene, so that her face rippled with pain at the crucial moment.

Imagine the uproar these days. Could anyone emerge from such a childhood unscathed?

17 NOVEMBER

Extremely murderous mood. Does PMT get worse as you get older? Sometimes I think it must. I barely noticed it in my twenties.

'Bring Tennis for lunch so he can play with the boys?' Eve texts, so we drive over to Camberwell. Their sitting room floor is covered with small plastic toys, so I spend most of the time sticking my fingers into his mouth to fish them out again.

18 NOVEMBER

Dennis is sick. When I opened his crate this morning, he whimpered and lay down instead of bounding out and prancing around my feet like normal. I carried him into the garden where he stood unhappily, shivering and eating grass.

We make yet another trip to the vet, who checks him out and says he seems fine, but gives him an anti-sickness injection (another £100).

He'd improved enough by the afternoon to go to the park, where a small plastic Pac-Man emerged from his bottom. He seemed very cheerful after that.

20 NOVEMBER

Drop Dennis off with Megan the dog sitter and head for Gatwick to fly to New York.

Finish Brooke's new book on the plane. There is a bizarre story in it about her labia, which I'll have to ask about, but the idea of quizzing Brooke Shields about this part of her anatomy over lunch in an Italian restaurant is quite daunting.

21 NOVEMBER

Brooke Shields is magnificent. She arrives at the hotel dressed entirely in black – black leggings, black cashmere hoodie, black overcoat – but with an enormous purple amethyst on her finger, a nod to the opening night she's attending later: *Death Becomes Her* on Broadway. Having been told that I only have an hour with her, she gives me four hours.

At one stage, discussing the labia story, she says the word 'labia' so loudly that the man on the sofa beside us looks a little startled.

Her labia were apparently 'uncomfortable', so after having her daughters, Brooke's gynaecologist recommended that she visit a surgeon in LA. The surgeon duly spent four hours 'down there', and when she came round, announced that not only had he reduced her labia, but he'd 'tightened' her up a bit too. 'After two kids, everything's looser,' he told Brooke with a wink, as if he'd done her an enormous favour.

What a creep. Also, she had her daughters by C-sections, so he really had no reason to be poking around down there. The guy should be in prison, I told her.

I end up in Brooke's enormous, blacked-out car, accompanying her through Manhattan to her next meeting. 'Do you have any plans to come to the UK soon?' I ask, and she replies that she's looking for a project. I remember that the script for my first novel has recently been finished, and explain that it features an American 50-something, the mother of the heroine, who has a breast cancer storyline.

'Send it to me,' says Brooke.

That night, having dinner with New York friends, I'm so excited by the prospect of Brooke Shields reading my film script that I drink three margaritas before dinner and then – exhausted and jet-lagged – almost fall asleep at the table.

22 NOVEMBER

Go to the Soho Hotel for a burger with the same friends before flying home. Benedict Cumberbatch walks in while we're eating. Google says he's six foot one but he looks much taller.

Halfway through lunch, I receive a text message about my flight being delayed for four hours due to a bomb scare at Gatwick, so we move to the bar and drink there for several hours. On his second gin martini, my friend Chris orders me a pillow and a blanket on an app called DoorDash, which is like Deliveroo, but for anything you want – not just food. Norse Atlantic doesn't offer passengers pillows or blankets for free, and Chris is worried I'm going to have an uncomfortable night flight otherwise.

Consequently, quite drunk, I struggle through security

at JFK carrying a pillow, and wearing my new blanket as a cape.

23 NOVEMBER

I land, pick a very excited Dennis up from Megan the dog sitter's house, and drive to Kent to stay with my stepsister Elizabeth for the weekend.

Dennis, unfortunately, lets us both down by doing a poo in her sitting room.

25 NOVEMBER

Email Brooke Shield's assistant the film script for my first book. 'It's *Saltburn* meets *Downton* meets *Fleabag* meets *The Devil Wears Prada*,' I tell her ambitiously.

'Are we still on for tomorrow?' texts the theatre director.

'We most certainly are,' I reply.

He suggests we have dinner before the stand-up, which makes me nervous. This feels suspiciously like a proper date.

26 NOVEMBER

A perfect winter day in the park – low sun, blue skies, leaves crisp underfoot. Dennis chases after a Pomeranian on our morning walk.

'He falls in love too easily,' jokes its owner as I try to get him back.

'Just like his owner,' I reply, although I don't think Dennis can have fallen in love with the Pomeranian. The thing has a fluffy tail like a duster and bulging eyes.

Over dinner with the theatre director, I laugh quite a lot. He's funny and very honest about relationships. He dates a lot, he says, and he sometimes dates those people for a relatively long time, but they're never exclusive. He never makes that promise. He had stage-four cancer when he was 28 and survived it; he's never married or had children. He hasn't led a conventional life, but he's interesting. Intriguing.

The stand-up is also very funny, although throughout the show I'm worrying about whether or not we'll kiss when we say goodbye. It's the second date, and kissing is expected on a second date, isn't it? But if we are going to kiss, where? On the street in Soho? Will I have to bend down?

We do kiss on the street in Soho, briefly, but it's a spectacularly bad, awkward kiss.

'Thank you for dinner,' I text him from the Tube. 'Although I feel like we're both better than that awkward kiss??'

By the time I get home, he's sent me a three-minute voice note in reply, which begins 'It was so awkward, I LOVED it.' This makes me laugh all over again.

27 NOVEMBER

I'm supposed to be going on another first date tonight, with a teacher from Hinge called Giles, but he messaged this morning cancelling it because 'things have moved rather quickly with someone else'. Sometimes, dating in London feels like racing for a fairground carousel and picking the first horse you see.

Maybe no bad thing to have a night in. If I start drying my hair and putting on mascara in the evening, Dennis has deciphered that this means I'm going out, and he lies on my bed looking sad.

Go to the butcher instead and buy some chicken thighs for me and a marrow bone for Dennis, then eat sticky, garlicky chicken in front of *Joy*, the new Netflix film about the invention of IVF, starring Thomasin McKenzie, James Norton and Bill Nighy. It makes me quite wish that Bill Nighy was my gynaecologist.

I think about my own frozen eggs, in a freezer at the Lister Hospital. If I was nearly ready to have a baby with Mike, would I think about having one by myself? I don't think so, I decide, watching Dennis push around his bone on the carpet. The responsibility of a puppy feels enough.

But at the same time, I feel a pang of sadness at giving up the idea of having one altogether, at having a different life to the majority of other women. I've long felt like an outlier among them – taller, more gawky, less romantically successful, less together, just *less*. Would not having children make me less, too? It feels like it, sometimes.

I text the director, thanking him for dinner, and he replies inviting me to a play about the IRA next week. Or, he says, I can come to his house and he'll cook. I pick the latter as fractionally more romantic.

December

Things I google in December:

- puppy ate a pine cone
- puppy housetrained at home but not other people's houses
- when did marx die
- how many christmas trees too many
- nigella ham cream pasta pea recipe
- can dogs have apple juice
- gipsy hill vet opening hours
- why do i miss my ex before my period
- how tall is apple martin
- can dogs have prunes
- why is my dog limping suddenly front leg
- pigs in blanket flavour crisps
- bromley christmas bin timetable

1 DECEMBER

Go into *The Telegraph* office to take calls for their annual Christmas charity phone-in. Readers call in to donate to the charities chosen by the newspaper; various writers come in to help take donations, usually including Richard Madeley and Rachel Johnson. Every caller wants to talk to the paper's star columnist, Allison Pearson, and sounds a bit disappointed when they get me. Often, if it's a male caller, he'll say, 'I don't read you, but my wife does.'

One man rings, I say my name, and he replies suspiciously, 'Don't you write a bit about your personal life?'

'Yes,' I admit, 'I have written a bit about my love life recently.'

'I thought the trouble was there isn't one!' he jokes back with a wheezy laugh.

All for a good cause, I remind myself.

2 DECEMBER

Go on a Hinge date with a Canadian accountant. Clever. Polite. Well-travelled. We have several glasses of wine in a peculiar Soho bar where they sell hard-boiled eggs from the counter, but I realize by our last round that I'm a tiny bit bored and want to get home to see Dennis.

3 DECEMBER

The Canadian accountant messages. 'Really enjoyed chatting and would be great to see you again if you're up for it.'

'I had a great time too, but will you forgive me if I say I didn't feel the dreaded "c word" (chemistry)?' I text back.

He doesn't reply.

4 DECEMBER

Meet a man who smokes a pipe while walking his Labrador, Floyd, in the park. He keeps his dog biscuits in his pocket in an old sock and says he always tries a new batch himself before giving them to Floyd. Are dog owners naturally more eccentric, or does having a dog make one more eccentric?

Head north to the director's house in Highgate for dinner. Having joked about how bad our kiss in the street was after dinner in Soho, we've joked about technique in subsequent messages and it's made me nervous. Wonder whether to take Dennis but decide that would only make me even less relaxed.

He cooks risotto and, afterwards, we sit on his sofa, kissing and jokily critiquing one another. It's funny, and lovely. Also, I can't help but notice that his bathroom has underfloor heating, which is a vast improvement on a building project in East London with a plastic loo.

When I leave, because I was always very clear that I'd need to get home to Dennis, the director gives me a party bag he made in advance because he was worried about the length of my journey to South London. It contains Reese's Pieces, a can of chocolate milk and a ginger shot.

'You are the loveliest man, thank you,' I text on the Tube.

But then, I thought Mike was a lovely man, and I fell for

that, too. How do you ever know? I feel too old to still be getting this wrong.

5 DECEMBER

My new vacuum arrives. After two months of deliberation, I've bought something called a 'Miele Cat & Dog' in the Black Friday sales. I trundle around my flat marvelling at its efficiency. Five power settings! Although I ignore the instructions about the suction strength of the highest setting and later notice several threads in my bathroom rug have come loose.

Go to a Christmas dinner party at my friend Amy's house in Vauxhall. Dress up in my new silver trousers and an off-the-shoulder top. Dennis does a poo on the way there, so I have to juggle my bag, my umbrella, a bottle of champagne, and various Christmas presents while trying to find a poo bag in the pouring rain.

We arrive looking like we've just trekked through the rainforest.

6 DECEMBER

The Times have asked me to interview Jillian Turecki. She's the world's biggest break-up coach, with nearly three million followers on Instagram, and a new self-help book coming out. She posts quotes online like 'Choose the one who chooses you back.' I would normally roll my eyes hard at this kind of truism, but given that I started following her on Instagram not long after the break-up, I say yes.

On our afternoon walk in the park, I get chatting to my neighbours, Eva and David, owners of Buddy, an elderly spaniel who doesn't like bicycles or skateboards. Eva tells me she makes something called liver cake as a dog treat. It's very easy, she insists: blend liver, egg and oats, and bake for half an hour or so. 'Some people use flour but someone in the know told me to use oats,' Eva says conspiratorially.

'But don't make it in the Nutribullet,' adds David, warning that it makes a very sticky paste that is impossible to clean off utensils. Apparently Eva uses a hand-held soup blender instead.

I walk home mulling over liver cake, but also thinking the point of a dog isn't just the dog. In the past four months, I've had multiple conversations a day with neighbours I would never have even wished good morning to before Dennis. You don't just get a dog, you get a community. I might have lost a boyfriend in the process, but it's beginning to feel like a good trade.

Three friends come for dinner, and I insist on getting out the Miele Cat & Dog to show them how good it is.

8 DECEMBER

Go out in the rain to buy a packet of lamb liver and a packet of duck liver. I don't need anything else, so I put both packets down on the Sainsbury's checkout like Hannibal Lecter, while everyone around me buys the Sunday papers and eggs.

At home, I blitz the livers, an egg and half a packet of oats in the Magimix. It makes a gloopy pink paste, which I pour into a cake tin and cook for forty-five minutes. When it comes out, it's so solid it could brain someone. Doesn't smell bad though. I'm almost tempted to try it. I've eaten worse. In Palermo, where they sell all sorts of offal in street markets, I once tried a small piece of calf's penis on a cocktail stick (very gristly).

9 DECEMBER

The liver cake's working. Dennis raced towards the ducks on the lake this morning, but I summoned him back by waving a piece.

I file my Brooke Shields interview, which covers ageing, her mother, her upbringing, her daughters, egg-freezing, her dog, and the intimate story of her labia reduction surgery.

11 DECEMBER

Go to a carol service in Chelsea in aid of the Marsden, with my two volunteering friends Jen and Lucy, plus their husbands.

Afterwards, we go to a French restaurant in Fulham for dinner and drink several bottles of red wine. The director and I text the whole way home in my Uber, and I invite him to my flat for dinner the following week. Our fourth date in nearly two months. This feels very slow, but maybe slow is good? It's very different to previous relationships, which I've rushed into, and subsequently decided I'm in love by date three. Falling in love too quickly is probably my main flaw. Or one of them, anyway.

12 DECEMBER

My editor emails about the Brooke interview. She doesn't understand the labia story. 'What exactly was wrong with it?'

I duly send the most embarrassing email of my professional life, asking Brooke Shields to clarify why she needed labia reduction surgery.

'I'm assuming it was, erm, larger?' I write.

She's never going to say yes to my film now.

13 DECEMBER

Dennis stuck his nose into a discarded KFC box in the park this morning, and by the afternoon was shivery, lethargic and ultimately sick on the kitchen floor. So back to the vet we go because I panicked that a bone might have become lodged somewhere. The vet gave him another anti-sickness injection and charged me another £100.

After the vet, I interviewed Jillian Turecki via Zoom. It was supposed to be about her new book, and being the world's most prominent break-up coach, but I talked quite a lot about my break-up and cried, which wasn't very professional.

Encouraged by Jillian, I block Mike afterwards on WhatsApp and Instagram, because he's been watching my stories and I find seeing his name on social media confusing.

Brooke Shield's assistant replies to my email. Can we say her labia was simply causing 'discomfort', she writes.

She adds that Brooke is going to read my script over the holidays.

I will be astonished if this comes to anything.

14 DECEMBER

Wake to a message from the theatre director: '*Slow Courting with Sophia*: a new podcast coming soon. Happy Saturday X'.

Dennis is recovered, which is lucky because we're meeting Eve and her boys in a Chelsea bakery for croissants and hot chocolate. Harry and Charlie fight over who gets to hold Dennis's lead, until they both drop it and Dennis runs through the café and outside, almost into the road.

I scream and run after him, but luckily a man outside put his foot on the lead, preventing Dennis from running under the wheels of a taxi. If this was a romcom, I think as I thank the man profusely while taking the lead back, we'd end up getting married with Dennis as our ring bearer. Unfortunately, the rescuer's wearing a tweed jacket and is about seventy. I'm all for an age gap but this is probably pushing it.

15 DECEMBER

Take Dennis on a walk around Nunhead Cemetery before lunch with a friend who lives nearby. Dennis pees on several gravestones. The youth of today have no respect.

Later, while scrabbling in my bedside table for a pair of earrings, I come across several old Post-it notes written by Mike that I'd stashed in the back of a drawer. Often, if I left the flat before he did in the morning, I'd come back to find notes saying 'I love you' or 'I miss you' stuck to my bathroom mirror or the shower door, and I squirrelled them away safely.

Burn them all in my log stove. Satisfying.

17 DECEMBER

Photoshoot for my *Times* interview with Jillian the break-up coach, because my editor wants a picture of me looking sad with Dennis to go with it.

The stylist puts me in a tight black dress that's slashed to the thigh, but I'm not allowed to smile because I need to appear heartbroken, so I end up looking like a sulky *Strictly* contestant.

Dennis chews a stiletto.

18 DECEMBER

Get Polly the hairdresser to turn me back to brunette. Blonde highlights suddenly feel too summery. I want a dark, glossy, enigmatic bob of the sort that 1960s stars might have worn under a Hermès headscarf with a pair of sunglasses.

When Polly pulls off the towel and dries it, I panic at the colour and feel like Morticia Addams with hair that's much too dark for my face, but I'm extremely polite and say I love it.

Finish the break-up piece on my laptop while in the hairdresser and send it to my editor at *The Times*.

19 DECEMBER

Breakfast meeting with a travel PR company to discuss returning to Florida next year and writing a piece entitled 'Is there more to Palm Beach than Trump?'.

We have eggs and bacon in a smart Jermyn Street restaurant and a woman behind us orders a dirty Martini at 10.30 a.m.

I suppose it is nearly Christmas. Very self-conscious of my new hair but I look less like Morticia Addams with enough bronzer on.

The director comes to Crystal Palace for our fourth date and produces a box of chocolates, a bag of marshmallows, a bottle of Baileys and a wrapped present from his rucksack. It's a small, second-hand book called *The Art of Kissing*, which he discovered online and bought me as a joke after our endless discussions about technique.

We have a drink and go to the cinema, then he comes back to mine for a glass of Baileys and more kissing on my sofa, although I make him get the last train north again. It's too soon to sleep with him because I still feel fragile, but I'm definitely also a bit smitten. How weird.

20 DECEMBER

Wake up with sore throat. Maybe from all the snogging. According to *The Times*, one in four people in London has the flu. It's that time of year, when everyone's already sick of drinking and hangovers and Slade on the radio, and we haven't even crawled home for Christmas yet.

21 DECEMBER

Feel like death but Dad and Shaunagh have booked tickets for us all to go to ABBA Voyage, so I drag myself there and manage to perk up for 'Mamma Mia' and 'Dancing Queen'.

Take Dennis for a brisk, cold walk around the block when

I get back, and we see Dash crouching under a car. I don't wish to be personal, but he looks as if he's put back on all those pounds that he lost. Too many Christmas party sausage rolls.

'Happy Christmas, Dash,' I say, as I pull Dennis away from him, desperate to get back into bed.

22 DECEMBER

Still ill, so I lie under my duvet all day watching a TV series about divorce lawyers. Wonder if I should have been one instead of a journalist because law looks much more financially stable and everyone seems to have excellent shoes.

The director invites me to stay at his house in Whitstable for a couple of nights between Christmas and New Year. I say yes and then worry about Dennis staying with him, too. It's not very sexy to get out of bed at 6.30 a.m. in the morning and say to your lover, 'I'm so sorry, I've just got to let my dog out so he can do a poo in your garden.'

23 DECEMBER

Drive to Mum's feeling as if I'm driving a sleigh. In the back of the car is: Dennis, my luggage, wellington boots, several wrapped presents, a case of champagne, a case of red wine, half a salmon, a Stilton, and a bag of Quality Street. Ho ho ho.

Settle down in front of *Corrie*. Gail's limbering up for her seventh wedding. Seems a bit unfair when some of us haven't even had one, I remark. Mum says there isn't enough money in the world to make her want seven husbands.

24 DECEMBER

Christmas Eve. Mum and I go to stay with her best friend for two nights. She has two Labradors, so Dennis and Beano lark around happily under the kitchen table while I wrap the dogs' presents. Beano is getting a stuffed crab; Dennis is getting a stuffed gingerbread man.

Am furious to discover that the bag of Quality Street I've bought contains only orange and strawberry cremes. They're selling bags of individual Quality Streets this year, and I didn't notice that when I grabbed this one in Sainsbury's. Do the police know about this?

25 DECEMBER

Christmas. The grandmother of the family we're staying with used to be a lady-in-waiting to the Queen, and was always given a box of royal crackers at Christmas. It was a perk for everyone who worked for the royals, apparently: all employees went home with the same crackers that the Queen had at Sandringham. Sadly, the King has stopped this practice, so we don't have any crackers at all.

Dennis prefers Beano's crab, so they fight over it until I confiscate both the crab and the gingerbread man.

Despite everything, because it's Christmas Day, because I drink too much red wine, because we talked of Christmases in the future, because I miss him, I think of Mike and wonder whether he's thinking of me. Overcome my aversion to orange and strawberry cremes and eat most of the Quality Street to distract myself.

26 DECEMBER

Mum and I drive back to her house and spend the entire day on the sofa watching the BBC drama about the creation of the SAS. It's brilliant – full of handsome young British actors motoring around the North African desert, saying things like, 'Let's win this fucking war.'

Eat a further ninety-six Quality Streets.

27 DECEMBER

Get up early and drive back to London from Mum's because I need to write my *Telegraph* column. I don't have many ideas because there isn't much in the paper. There never is at this time of year because newspapers are operating with skeleton staff and the main stories tend to be about whatever Kate Middleton was wearing at church on Christmas Day. Luckily, my editor allows me to write about the SAS, a tongue-in-cheek column about the days when men could be men, in which I include an anecdote about an SAS commander I once dated.

He was extremely handsome, very charming, and had a gravelly voice like James Bond, I write. We went out for several dinners and he joked about me becoming his second wife. I was quite seduced by this idea, until I discovered that he was wooing another Sophia at the same time (this was when I was working for *Tatler*, and Sophias were two a penny). 'Perhaps these rogues are better in fiction than in real life,' I conclude in my column.

As I turn 40 in a couple of months, that's what I'm telling myself anyway: no more rogues.

29 DECEMBER

Drive to Whitstable to stay with the director. Booked a nearby dog sitter for Dennis in the end, deciding this was easier than having him with me. Don't tell Mum because she'll think it's neglectful to leave Dennis with a stranger so I can go off and have a romantic minibreak.

His house is amazing – an old cottage with a contemporary ground-floor glass extension and great art on the walls.

Having discussed his snoring in advance, I leave his room when we go to sleep and settle down in the spare room. It is – technically – the first night we've spent together, albeit in separate bedrooms like a Victorian couple. But I've always found sleeping beside someone for the first time alarming – what if you need to get up and pee in the night? What if you accidentally fart in bed? – so it feels like the perfect compromise.

30 DECEMBER

Wake up to a WhatsApp from the director. 'Tea?' I get up and go back to his room, and we have tea in bed before taking a long walk along the beach in the watery December sunshine, discussing dating, how I feel three months on from my break-up, and what's happening with us.

What's happening with 'us' seems to be a vague, nebulous thing. We enjoy hanging out with one another. We make one another laugh. But I can't resolve two thoughts in my head – he's 57 and he doesn't do exclusive relationships. So if I want a relationship, and if I want children, why am

I doing this at all? Given that I'm nearly 40, it could be wasting time.

Or maybe it's enough to be having a nice time with someone right now.

31 DECEMBER

I sneak out of the spare room early, tiptoe into the director's room and kiss him goodbye, before getting in the car, picking up Dennis from the dog sitter and driving to Wales for a New Year's Eve party organized by my friend Cleo, who used to work for Boris Johnson.

Her brother lives in a beautiful, old house overlooking the Brecon Beacons, and twenty of us gather downstairs that evening for champagne in black tie. There are two other dogs – Cleo's bulldog, Hippo, and a Labrador puppy called Steve. The three of them spend all night under our feet, humping one another. 'It's like *The Human Centipede*,' someone jokes at one stage.

Just after midnight, I check my phone to see that the director has messaged saying 'Happy New Year', and I feel giddy. But am I letting my head run away with itself all over again?

January

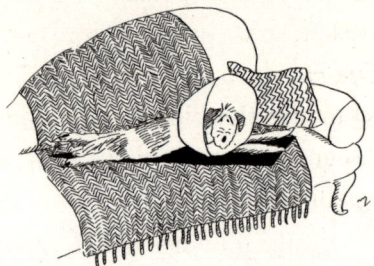

Things I google in January:

- why are my soaked beans still hard
- dog needy after neuter
- how many dogs does carole middleton have
- do dogs get depression
- ovary throbbing
- how many units 250ml wine
- dog limping front leg
- tablespoon sunflower seeds how many calories
- is chicken stock good for dogs
- how many times does the average person fall in love
- bromley bins missed collection

1 JANUARY

Cleo and I take Hippo and Dennis for a bracing walk in the Brecon Beacons. I lose all feeling in my fingers and Dennis strains at the lead, panting like a pitbull on account of the nearby sheep. Only five of us left in the house that evening as various others have left, so we polish off the champagne on the sofa in front of *Die Hard with a Vengeance*. I had a teenage crush on Alan Rickman in this film, which could explain quite a lot about my subsequent romantic choices, given that he plays a maniac with appalling peroxide hair.

2 JANUARY

'Are you still in Wales?' the director texts, shortly after I leave the house in the morning.

'Wending my way home this very second,' I dictate to my phone.

'I don't like the idea of you driving and texting,' he replies, which makes me smile because it implies he cares.

Oh God, I *am* falling for this man who's explicitly stated he doesn't do exclusive relationships! Will I literally never learn?

3 JANUARY

Dennis and I have been commissioned by *The Times* to visit various restaurants and see how dog-friendly they are. First up, a café in Chelsea, where a nice woman called Norma brings me a coffee and a croissant, and Dennis a bowl of water and platter of carrots. For lunch, we go to Chucs in Mayfair, where Dennis jumps on to the velvet banquette. When the waitress brings over some complementary truffled arancini balls, I surreptitiously feed him one. Dennis's first truffle.

'Do you get lots of dogs in here?' I ask. She nods and then tells me they sometimes get cats at the branch in Chelsea. Who would bring their cat to a restaurant, I think, as I feed Dennis another arancini ball. *Weirdos.*

That evening, we meet Eve at an Italian on the Fulham Road. Dennis does a poo under the decorative olive tree outside as we arrive, then flops under the table, exhausted by his day of eating and criss-crossing London. Lucio, the restaurant owner, says customers often buy the fillet steak (£48.50) and share it with their dogs. I mustn't become that person, I tell myself, as I tear off a piece of focaccia and drop it under the tablecloth.

4 JANUARY

My *Times* interview with the break-up guru is out, and there's a big picture of me on the front page looking quite masculine (severe jawline), under a huge headline that says 'CAN I MEND MY BROKEN HEART?'

Sometimes I reckon it might have been an easier life as a proctologist or a firefighter.

Get the Tube to Highgate for dinner with the director, although he has a bad cold and insists on no contact so I don't catch it. We play backgammon across the sofa while a piece of pork cooks in the oven. Funny how dating changes. In my twenties, it meant several bottles of wine and a sloppy lunge in a pub. Now it's chaste boardgames and a roast dinner.

It starts snowing just before I head home, so I slide down the streets of Highgate towards the Tube station.

5 JANUARY

Go to Sainsbury's to buy papers and the week's groceries – largely fruit and vegetables to make up for Christmas overindulgence. Several other shoppers lurk in the nuts aisle, looking sad and confused.

The director and I text all day, back and forth. 'I think slow is good,' he says, when we discuss the fact we can't see each other for another two weeks. 'And you're dating other people, right?' he adds, laughing, at the end of a voice note.

I keep opening Hinge and scrolling through other men, but I'm not sure I'm the kind of person who can be sleeping with someone while dating others. I feel as if I've accidentally stumbled into one of those modern relationships you increasingly read about these days – some sort of polyamorous situation – whereas I want to swoon over and feel crazy about just one person. 'You're such a *romantic*,' the director has said several times, as if that's a bad thing. But is wanting to be with just one person such a bad, old-fashioned, unworkable idea?

Take Dennis for another walk in the park before it gets dark. Increasingly, I can see why people become 'dog people' or 'cat people'. Animal relationships are more straightforward than human ones. It's a purer, easier kind of love.

6 JANUARY

I take back what I said about it being an easier kind of love.
Dennis makes the first Monday morning in January even less
enjoyable by running off and refusing to come back in the park.

'Sorry, so sorry! He's a puppy!' I shout at one woman,
whose elderly beagle was aggressively humped. The internet
told me this would start happening around now because he's
reaching 'sexual maturity', but it's not very relaxing for other
dogs (or me) at 7 a.m.

Back home, I ring the vet and make his neutering appointment. Dennis sits at my feet while I'm on the phone, looking up
at me, tail thumping on the kitchen floor, and I feel so guilty
I have to screw my eyes closed as I confirm the date.

7 JANUARY

Lily Allen's husband has cheated on her using the celebrity
dating app Raya. According to *The Sun*, she found out by
creating a fake profile herself and then discovering his. Poor
Lily. It reminds me of the time, many years ago, when I messaged a Stringfellows dancer on Instagram and found out an
ex-boyfriend was cheating on me. He'd been liking her pictures
but insisted nothing was going on, so I got in touch with her,
she confirmed the opposite and I felt my heart crack. I'd been
so sure of him until suddenly I wasn't.

It's easy to become an internet sleuth if you suspect
something, these days. When I wrote my fifth novel, about
a private detective who specializes in affairs, I had a terrific
time researching the ways people catch out their other halves.

My favourite remains the woman who suspected something was up when she discovered a footprint on the inside of her car windscreen.

8 JANUARY

Drive to Mum's to drop off Dennis because I'm off to Spain with Rosie for a weekend with Dad. Shaunagh's in Tenerife for ten days, so we're going to keep him company for a few days.

I update her on the director. 'I like him,' I tell her, 'but the whole non-exclusive thing …'

'Just see,' she advises. 'If you're having a nice time, great. And if that changes down the line, then you look at it.'

It seems so simple when other people give you advice.

There's been a stabbing in *Corrie*. 'That's all we need,' Mum says with a tut, as if she lives on the street herself.

9 JANUARY

'I've put you in a different bedroom to last time,' Dad says, as he carries my bag upstairs. He means the last time I was here with Mike, in August, when we drove to Spain with Dennis.

In the garden, I look around and feel a small pang, then Dad appears in the sunshine holding up a bottle of cold rosé. 'Drinks time,' he announces.

He, Rosie and I sit in the January sunshine, under the orange blossom, and eat jamón and olives while finishing the bottle. New memories to override the old.

10 JANUARY

We go on a bike ride through the Spanish countryside, Dad leading from the front. Rosie and I have borrowed padded cycling shorts from Shaunagh's wardrobe and childishly can't stop laughing at each other's bottoms.

Later, she and I play backgammon, and I send the director a photo of the board, demonstrating that I beat her.

'You having fun?'

'Yeah,' I text back. 'Obviously I wouldn't publicly admit this, but I've thought about you a few times.'

'Your secret's safe with me,' he answers. 'I admit that you've been more than a fleeting thought in my mind.'

My heart swoons a bit at this.

11 JANUARY

Mum sends me a photo of Dennis sitting on a chair at the kitchen table, looking forlornly at a batch of freshly baked cookies, as if he's Oliver Twist and been told he can't have any more.

12 JANUARY

My interview with Brooke Shields is on the front page of the *Mail on Sunday*. 'Brooke Shields's shock discovery as she woke up from intimate op' is the headline. No word about my film script. I think we can take it as a no.

Fly back from Barcelona and drive to Mum's where Dennis bounces all over me. He was a very good boy, apparently, although he also chewed her hairbrush, tried to get into the biscuit cupboard, chewed the head off Beano's favourite toy and did a little poo in her bedroom. Fortunately, like a benevolent grandmother, Mum forgives these transgressions.

13 JANUARY

Leave Sussex at 5 a.m. to drive home in time to tear through all the papers and email my *Telegraph* editor some column ideas. Accidentally shunt into the back of a woman's Nissan half a mile from my flat. Climb out, in the middle of rush hour traffic, honking all around, and apologize, feeling guilty, and also deranged with tiredness after all the travel of the past few days. There's a scratch to her car and small dent to mine. What a start to a Monday. Dennis watches, confused, from the passenger seat.

'This north–south divide is annoying,' the director texts from Highgate when I update him, 'otherwise I'd come and make you a cup of tea.'

14 JANUARY

My neighbour Larry comes over for a drink. I've seen him from time to time in the street, and we've grimaced at one another in the way that London people do – 'I'm acknowledging that I live next door to you, but this doesn't mean we have to be friends.' But last week Larry stopped and bent down to pat Dennis, and said if I ever needed a dog sitter, he'd be very happy to have him. Now he's coming round to meet him properly.

Larry – 50-something, very chatty, wildly camp – encourages

me to tell him everything about my love life, so I fill him in while Dennis sleeps on his lap in front of the log stove.

'This all sounds extremely unhealthy,' he says of the director. 'But when I had my last boyfriend they were still riding horses in the streets, so what do I know?'

He hands a sleepy Dennis over to me as he leaves. 'Uncle Larry will have you to stay any time.'

I smile as I close the door behind him. A new neighbour friend, all thanks to Dennis.

15 JANUARY

Have lunch in a vegan café near Holborn with my first ever boyfriend so he can hand over a bag of ceramic plates from Romania. Garrett was my university tutor, American, older than me, but we remained friends after we split, and he stayed in touch with Dad and Shaunagh. We all stayed in such close contact, in fact, that he and a subsequent girlfriend got married at their house in Spain.

My parents recently visited Garrett at his holiday home in Romania, and now he's delivering a very heavy bag of ceramic plates Shaunagh ordered from a local potter. Like a drug mule, except instead of handing over packets of heroin it's pretty green and white plates. At least I hope it's plates. I update him on Mike and the director, and he shows me photos of his children. I sit across the table and wonder what my life would have looked like if we'd stayed together, how many heartbreaks I might have avoided. A more straightforward life, maybe, but where's the fun in that?

Also, I think as I lug the ceramics home, I'd never have found Dennis.

16 JANUARY

Dennis, on the lead, is suddenly aggressive towards a spaniel puppy in the park, leaping on it and snarling. I pull him off, stutter apologies, and tell the owner he's being neutered next week.

I growl at him as we walk off and he gives me a look that says 'So what? You're not the boss of me.'

This incident makes me feel even less warmly towards the idea of having children.

18 JANUARY

Have three journalist friends over for lunch. Sophie (aged 45) falls through the door saying she's tired from an exhausting night with a 22-year-old Hinge date. We eat ox cheek stew around my kitchen table while discussing the merits of younger men ('Enthusiasm,' Sophie says), and gossiping about other journalists.

After they leave, I make the spare bed before the director arrives. His first overnight stay here. He arrives with chocolates, which we eat in front of the fire.

Dennis would make a terrible guard dog because he's all over this strange new man in the house. Not remotely suspicious.

I wake at 2.30 a.m. and sneak out to the spare bedroom on account of the director's snoring.

19 JANUARY

'Room service?' says a WhatsApp from the director at 8.02 a.m., so I go into my bedroom with mugs of tea, followed by Dennis.

When the director and I begin kissing, he pulls back and frowns.

'What?' I said, worrying that my breath smells.

'Dennis is licking my leg,' he replies.

I put Dennis in his crate for the next hour. I cannot have sex while being watched by my dog.

20 JANUARY

The local Facebook group has kicked off. Apparently, a dog called Patrick attacked another dog, and Patrick's owner did very little to help the situation. Dozens of locals are now calling for dogs to be on leads permanently in the park.

'It really bothers me when dogs are let off their lead when they're not trained,' writes one, which makes me feel guilty. Dennis is off the lead and scampers up to other dogs a lot, but if I never let him off, how will he learn to come back?

'Who the fuck names their dog Patrick?' writes someone else.

21 JANUARY

'I'm so sorry, he's getting the snip tomorrow,' I tell another dog walker, whose labradoodle was humped before breakfast this morning. I'm not sure there's a single person within a five-mile radius of the park who doesn't know about this operation by now.

Back home, I record a segment for the *Spectator* podcast via Zoom. This week's issue has an article about the depressing reality of sex parties, so they've asked me on because I once wrote about the subject for *Tatler*.

It was in 2015, not long before the first *Fifty Shades of Grey* film was released and, as research for my article, I went to a fetish party on a barge on the Thames (with Eve for safety). She wore lingerie; I wore a latex catsuit. We drank prosecco at the bar nervously until a man in lederhosen, a collar and a lead approached us and declared that he wanted to be our slave for the night. Eve made him get down on his hands and his knees and act as our 'table'.

'Go on, Soph, put your boots on his back!' she instructed.

So I did, and she did, and we sat there drinking prosecco with our heels on this man's bare back. Later, we went below deck to an area where various apparatuses were set up for spanking, and watched curiously from the sidelines. It smelled of sex and hormones.

My uncle used to run a company that provided nightclub security, I tell the podcast, and he says it was much better in the days when smoking was allowed inside, because cigarettes masked the smell of body odour.

22 JANUARY

Drive Dennis to the vet feeling like I'm carting him to the gallows, particularly as he hasn't been allowed breakfast ahead of the operation and keeps looking at me with extreme sadness from the passenger seat.

Martin the vet needed his exact weight for the anaesthetic, but Dennis wouldn't stand still on the scales. Unfortunately, this meant I had to get on the scales – first by myself, then holding Dennis – so we could work out the difference, and thus what Dennis weighs. 'This is very unfair after Christmas,' I grumbled, which Martin seemed to find amusing.

Leave Dennis looking pitiful and drive home, via the butcher, almost crying.

'Can I have a marrow bone for my dog? He's getting castrated today,' I tell the butcher, who visibly shudders and hurries out the back to fetch one.

At tea-time, the receptionist rings, saying the operation's been a success and Dennis is ready to be picked up. I hurry there and want to both laugh and cry when he waddles into the reception with a plastic cone around his neck. Carefully, I scoop him up and carry him to the car.

It's like driving home someone who's recently been concussed, the cone swaying backwards and forwards on the seat beside me.

Back home, he doesn't want any food, and we have a quiet evening on the sofa in front of the telly. I sneak a look at the wound and his stitches, and want to cry all over again. I feel like I've lobotomized him.

23 JANUARY

Bad night. I dragged his crate into my room so Dennis could sleep near me, but he kept whimpering inside it. Martin said anaesthetic can cause confusion, so in the end I gave up with the crate and lifted him on to my bed, trying to overlook my neurosis that his stitches would leak on my expensive Beata Heuman quilt.

At 5 a.m., I gave up trying to sleep and carried him out to the garden for a wee. He'd perked up enough to eat something by lunchtime, and soon after that worked out how to wriggle out of the cone, so back to the vet we went for a turquoise onesie, to stop him from getting to his stitches.

A plumber comes over to fix a leak in my cellar and winces in sympathy when I tell him why Dennis is dressed like a Smurf. Then he takes out his phone and shows me a photo of his dog, an XL bully called Ailsa. Ailsa looks like she'd eat newborn babies for breakfast.

'Good as gold,' he says proudly.

24 JANUARY

Relinquish nurse duties and leave Dennis on my bed in his Smurf-suit for a gym class at lunchtime. When I get back, he crawls into my lap like a toddler who needs a hug. This makes me cry (again).

25 JANUARY

We go outside for a potter on the lead, very slowly, so Dennis doesn't burst his stitches, then catch the train to a Herne Hill pub to meet two old journalist friends.

After a tough week, Dennis is delighted to be the centre of attention in the pub. I tell a middle-aged woman that he's just been neutered and she gives him a sympathetic look. 'Much easier without them, darlin', I say that to my husband all the time.'

26 JANUARY

Very January weather. It's as if the day can't quite be bothered to get light. Leave Dennis with Larry the Neighbour because I feel too stressed about the idea of taking him to the director's immaculate house.

Larry opens his front door and snatches Dennis's lead. 'Hello, gorgeous, come in quick,' he says, in extreme camp mode. 'Mummy's off to see her terrible boyfriend.'

'Not boyfriend, but thank you,' I shout over my shoulder as I run for the train.

The director and I walk to a nearby pub for lunch and dance around the subject of going away together in the summer. Will this strange, non-exclusive, non-relationship relationship still be rumbling on by then? I like the idea at the same time as being confused by it. Can I really go on holiday with a man who's dating other women?

27 JANUARY

Agree to write a piece in tribute to Carole Middleton for the *Mail*. She's turning 70. Don't have much intel on her, although a friend who was on holiday in Mustique at the same time as the whole family a couple of years ago told me that Prince Louis was a terror on the beach one afternoon, and refused to get out of the sea. 'Go away, you're old!' my friend heard him tell his granny Carole, as she tried to cajole him out. Stick that detail in my piece. To think I once wanted to be a war reporter.

Another menacing post about dogs has appeared on the local Facebook group. Someone's conducted a poll asking if all dogs should be on leads, and 72 per cent have said they should.

'Dogs should be forced to wear nappies while they're at it,' says a comment underneath. 'I'm sick of my sneakers being ruined.'

'You want the country's landfill sites to be filled with dog nappies, do you?' writes another local.

Wonder if the country turning dog-mad during Covid means that those who don't like dogs have become more trenchant, too. Dog people versus anti-dog people. Yet another schism, as with Brexit and the Covid vaccine. Potential war over dog poo and uncontrollable terriers who chase squirrels.

28 JANUARY

Gynaecological ultrasound at Croydon Hospital to check a niggling ovary pain I've had for a few weeks. As usual, get lost in its impenetrable corridors.

'Hello, darling, come in,' says a large, jolly nurse when

I finally find the right department and am called into a room. She goes through the usual procedure of telling me to pop my clothes on the chair and my 'bottom on the end of the bed. Scoot down, scoot down, scoo— That's it.'

I lie back nervously. Given Mum's eleven-year ordeal with ovarian cancer, any gynaecological pain makes me anxious.

'So you've had a cyst before?' the nurse asks, as she frowns at her computer screen.

'Mmhmm,' I reply.

She spends five minutes clicking away, taking measurements.

'Can you see anything?' I pluck up the courage to ask.

'You'll get the results in five days,' she tells me.

'You can't tell me anything now?'

'You'll get the results in five days,' she says again, with a smile.

Spend the drive home trying to work out whether it was a 'you-have-ovarian-cancer' smile, or a 'you-have-nothing-to-worry-about' smile.

29 JANUARY

My friend Hannah, a beauty writer, invites me to a posh hotel dinner for the launch of a £900 perfume. The French perfume designer sits at the front of the room and talks about the quality of its rose petals. It smells like rich old lady. We're all given a bottle in a goody bag to take home. Wonder if I should keep it or sell it on eBay to cover Dennis's biscuits, treats, chews, toys, and vet bills.

30 JANUARY

Having a dog makes you more aware of the light. Dennis and I can now be in the park just before 7 a.m. instead of having to wait for another half an hour, as we did in the thick of December. There are primroses poking up under the old oak trees and robins hopping between them, until Dennis bounds along and scatters the birds into the air.

The same applies to the afternoons. We can leave later and dally in the park until 5 p.m. Every extra minute of light feels like a victory. I'm pretty sure Dennis isn't aware of the Earth's axial tilt and the slow approach of spring, but I'm grateful to him for showing me that the darkness is sliding behind us for another season.

31 JANUARY

Back to the vet for the final check. 'Oh, that's healed very well. That looks *lovely*,' says Martin, inspecting Dennis's withered scrotum.

February

Things I google in February:

- dog ate razor clam shell ok
- how to cook lamb chops
- famous hermits
- what to do when your dog looks bored
- why do dogs roll in dead things
- best vegetables in february
- why is marmalade so popular in japan
- can dogs eat old cow bones
- what did jane austen die of
- best tinted moisturiser for older skin
- history of the crumpet
- how to stop dog chasing sheep

1 FEBRUARY

Go to see *Ballet Shoes* at the National Theatre with the director. Am distracted from the loveliness of the play by a weirdness between us. He barely touches me, and as we're queuing to leave the theatre, he taps at his phone and I see Hinge suggested as one of his most-used apps, which makes my stomach drop.

Have a cup of tea afterwards in the BFI café, surrounded by nerds dressed as Doctor Who, but I make polite conversation instead of saying what I really want to, which is 'What are we doing?' We eat in restaurants together, go to the theatre together, sleep together, but we're not really together. Go home sad, the same thought rolling around my head like a marble – *can I do this?*

2 FEBRUARY

Lunch for Dad's seventieth in a Belgravia pub. Leave Dennis with Larry the Neighbour. ('Mummy's off drinking again, isn't she, sweetheart?' he tells him with a theatrical sigh on his doorstep.)

My siblings and I perform a poem that mentions Rod Stewart, Dad's passion for sailing and cycling, and a memorable game of charades, in which a cheeky teenage friend of ours gave Shaunagh 'Free Willy', so she retaliated by giving him 'Deep Throat'. I do think it's a miracle that we've grown up semi-normal, sometimes.

Feel spike of anxiety when I see a missed call from Larry

halfway through lunch and assume he's killed Dennis. Why else would he be interrupting my dad's seventieth?

Text him back under the table. 'You alright?'

'No need to panic,' he replies. 'It was a question about his lead, but Uncle Larry's sorted it.'

3 FEBRUARY

Follow Dennis down a grassy bank in the park this morning and slip and fall on a dog poo, which somehow covers my leggings and smears itself under my coat and up my back.

Later, I send the director an awkward voice note, saying that the past few days have been tricky for me, and that I'm feeling a bit contemplative about our situation. He sends me one back (six minutes! Psychopath!), saying that he gets it. 'I think that it's helpful and not helpful to date someone like me after the kind of break-up you've been through,' he says. 'Your description of your year with Mike ... there's a lot to unpack there. You're still sort of grieving and working out what all that was.'

Am I? Maybe. Maybe it's too early to be in another relationship. Maybe I should just be with one man for a bit: Dennis.

4 FEBRUARY

Crouch on the pavement for several minutes on the way to the park, trying to prise a chicken bone from Dennis's mouth. If I was prime minister, people who discard chicken bones in the street would get life sentences.

Write my Substack on the grimness of this year's Valentine's cards. They're worse than ever. 'You blow me away,' says one, illustrated with a cartoon bottom and a fart bubble.

Debate whether to send the director a card. Last year, Mike cooked a seabass for us at home. But what do you do with a man with whom you're in a non-exclusive relationship? Google 'Arsenal Valentine's cards' and find one with Bukayo Saka on the front, above the caption 'You're great in the Saka'. Order it.

Have dinner at Eve's. At her therapist's suggestion, she's started writing down a list of daily pet peeves that annoy her in a Notes document on her phone. The list so far includes 'shooing a pigeon and it not moving', 'anyone who calls a pain-au-chocolat a chocolate croissant', and the word 'holibobs'.

Dennis emerges from her utility room with a pair of her pants in his mouth.

5 FEBRUARY

While walking around the lake in the park, I listened to a report on Radio 4 about the world's first lab-grown dog food, which is going on sale in the UK this week. It's grown from chicken cells. They interview various dog owners who sound very suspicious.

Dennis licks a dirty tissue, and I wonder whether we should be that neurotic about what our dogs eat, given that most of them like any old rubbish they can get from the pavement.

Eve texts me another pet peeve: 'That momentary panic when Apple automatically generates an extremely complicated suggested password and you briefly think it's going to be your new password.'

6 FEBRUARY

Breathless phone call from a *Sunday Times* editor, asking if I can test the lab-grown dog food on Dennis and write a review for this weekend's paper. Spend most of day trying to get hold of a bag from a pet superstore in Brentford. Go to a posh pet shop in Clapham to find the silliest dog treats I can. They have quail treats, pheasant biscuits and venison chipolatas, and I buy them all to test on Dennis. The PR for the lab-grown dog food bikes me over a bag of the treats from Brentford, and I try a rigorous and scientific test of all the treats, making Dennis sit for them in the garden.

He wolfs them all down, including the lab-grown biscuits, and doesn't seem to prefer one over another. Write my piece for the *Sunday Times*, pointing out that it's not the dogs that are picky about what they eat – it's their owners.

8 FEBRUARY

Drive to Whitstable for the weekend with the director. We go for a stroll along the harbour, then watch a film in bed. Later, he takes me out for an advance birthday dinner because I'm going to be away for the big day. We eat moules and share a bottle of wine across a table with a candle on it. 'It's almost romantic,' I joke, and he widens his eyes in pretend panic.

At least I think it's pretend.

9 FEBRUARY

Breakfast in a Whitstable café that has seashells, driftwood and local art for sale on the walls. Walk back to the director's house via Co-Op to get the papers. The *Sunday Times* editor liked my dog food story and has moved it from the back of the paper to the third page, with a photo Mike took of me and Dennis on the day we brought him home. I'm beaming, carrying Dennis in a bag under my arm because he hadn't had his jabs and couldn't be put down on the pavement. It was taken only seven months ago, but it feels like a century.

As I drive home, Dennis on the passenger seat beside me, I think about then and now. I was so convinced that was the right relationship with Mike, and I got it so wrong, and I'm very unsure about what's going on with the director, but I really like him. He's kind, generous, funny, and very open about his feelings whenever we check in with where we're at. He said this weekend that he isn't 'quite ready' to stick an exclusive label on us yet, but then I'm not, either.

We seem to have accidentally fallen into this place where we like each other a lot, we like hanging out with one another, making one another laugh, we like being draped over one another in bed watching television, so maybe we don't need to call it anything. Maybe right now, this is enough. Maybe these modern, open relationships aren't so bad?

10 FEBRUARY

Dennis has learned that neighbourhood cats lurk underneath cars and insists on stopping to look, walk around and sniff under each one on the walk home from the park, like an officious policeman. Realize we haven't seen fat Dash for several weeks. Wonder if they've moved, or if he's been put on such a stringent post-Christmas diet that he's wasted away. I hope he's OK.

Getting a dog has made me feel more sympathetic towards other pet owners, I realize, whether they have a dog or a cat. I may even feel more understanding of those weirdos who have snakes or tarantulas. Whether it's a hairy terrier or a hairy spider, they're still our little creatures. Ours to look after. Please let Dash be alright.

11 FEBRUARY

Ring the doctor to chase up my gynaecological scan results. They said I'd hear within five days and I haven't. I've been assuming no news is good news, but thought I should probably check.

'Ah, yes,' says the GP receptionist, after I give her my details. 'The doctor *does* want to talk to you.'

Oh God, I think, my stomach spinning. Perhaps I do have ovarian cancer. There has to be something, otherwise why would the doctor want to talk? The GP will ring the following day, adds the receptionist. This means a whole day of worrying.

Distract myself by writing a column about the country's

dog poo epidemic. In parts of Shropshire, complaints about 'dog fouling' have increased over 200 per cent in the past two years. It's not stated whether the residents of Shropshire are particularly lazy. Instead, the pandemic puppy-boom is blamed.

I go online and discover the problem is often worse during winter, when it's dark, because people leave their dog poo on the streets in the belief that nobody will see them ignoring it. Old people are also blamed by various internet threads, because they're deemed too infirm to bend down. Is this fair? The old Queen was still riding into her nineties. Not that she probably ever had to pick up poo from a pavement.

12 FEBRUARY

The doctor calls first thing and says I have two haemorrhagic cysts on my left ovary, roughly the size of broad beans. 'Haemorrhagic' means full of blood, Google says. Revolting.

'Two cysts, nothing more dramatic,' I text Rosie.

'PHEW,' she replies. 'Do they want to remove them, or can they just stick around?'

'Nah, another scan in six months to check them,' I text back.

'OK, but can our uteruses actually get a grip,' she replies. 'Being a woman is EXHAUSTING.'

Go to Claridge's for dinner with an old friend because I'm writing a piece about crumpets becoming fashionable again for a magazine, and Claridge's have crumpets on the menu as an amuse-bouche. Two, smallish crumpets, covered with Welsh cheddar and thin slivers of black truffle. Kate Moss comes out of the hotel bar as we arrive. Very thin. Don't imagine she's ever eaten a crumpet.

13 FEBRUARY

Eve takes me out for a pre-birthday dinner. First to The Langham for a drink, then to a trendy Marylebone restaurant called Lita, which has just been awarded a Michelin star. It's full of men who look like they work at hedge funds and women who look like they're married to men who work at hedge funds. This makes sense when I look at the menu and realize every main course is at least £50. We could share a turbot for £160 or, if we were feeling Tudor, a rib of beef, also for £160.

'Still or sparkl—' began our waiter.

'TAP IS FINE!' I screeched, already totting up the bill in my head.

'And do you maybe want to begin with a glass of champag—'

'No! Just wine,' I say quickly.

It was delicious – we ate tuna sashimi, and a small bowl of duck ragu, and shared a pork chop, which arrived at the table like still life, beautifully coloured with slices of peach and apple, salad leaves, and capers. Plus a side of potatoes (for £8!). Eve's added another pet peeve to her list – anyone who cannot get through an anecdote without getting out their phone to show you a meme or a video on YouTube.

The bill was £300 in the end, and I couldn't let her pay for both of us. London restaurants have become crazy – and yet they're also full of people who seem to think nothing of spending £50 on a main course. I don't wish to sound ungrateful, but I'd rather be at home with a bowl of pasta (and Dennis) than sitting at a table, worrying about what the bill is going to come to. Another sign of age, I suspect.

14 FEBRUARY

Up at 5 a.m. to drive to the Lake District for a weekend of judging entries ahead of the World Marmalade Awards. This has been an annual event since 2005, held at a stately home just outside Penrith, entered into by thousands of amateur and professional marmalade makers from around the world. I've written about the awards before, but this year I've been invited to judge the entries, ahead of the festival weekend in April, and write another piece about it for the *Times*. Two days. Hundreds of jars of marmalade. A lot of sugar.

Mum has already sent me a cautionary text. 'Careful with driving afterwards. I read somewhere that judges eat so much sugar they can slip into diabetic comas.'

Dennis isn't allowed at the stately home, so I've found a local dog sitter called James who lives nearby and, after six hours on the motorway, hand him over in a Penrith petrol station car park like a hostage.

Arrive at the house and am shown to my room. I'm sleeping in a four-poster bed that was given to the family by Queen Anne. There are three old woollen blankets piled at the end because this house is freezing. If possible, I think it might be colder inside than outside. 'Bring warm clothes,' the organizers emailed us in advance. No kidding.

Put on two jumpers and go down to the kitchen for dinner with some of the other judges, who are drinking red wine and huddled in front of the Aga. They include a food writer I know; the renowned food historian Ivan Day; Karen Jankel, the daughter of the *Paddington* writer; plus a Japanese tea master dressed in a ceremonial kimono, which cannot be possibly warm enough.

'OH JESUS!' the director texts me, having opened his Valentine's card with Bukayo Saka on the front of it. 'You total romantic. Thank you, baby.'

'I don't know what you're talking about,' I reply, trying to ignore how delighted I am by him calling me baby.

15 FEBRUARY

Two of the judges come down to breakfast this morning in their coats. 'Ah yes,' says Bea, the daughter of the couple who own the house. 'They were in the attic. I thought they might be chilly.'

We encourage circulation back into our fingers by buttering toast and gripping mugs of steaming coffee, and then begins the serious business of judging.

This takes place around a large table in the dining room (warmed by a fire). At each judge's place is a pen, a stack of marking sheets, several marmalade entries, and a lamp so we can inspect the clarity and set of each jar. In the middle of the table are boxes marked 'CLEAN' and 'DIRTY' for the tasting spoons, jugs of water, and boxes of Carr's water biscuits, which can be used as palate cleansers. Around the edges of the room are thousands of jars of marmalade, neatly stacked in crates.

As a newbie, I've been seated beside Will, a chef and buyer for Waitrose's pudding department, who's judged here before. From a stack of jars in front of us, he picks a jar of yuzu marmalade from Japan and opens it. We both try a spoonful, then throw our spoons in the 'DIRTY' box, then take two more spoons from the 'CLEAN' box and try it again. Will decides it has a decent colour and level of bitterness, but the peel is slightly chewy, so awards it 17 out of 20.

Spend the rest of the day judging jars by myself, my cheeks flushing as my sugar levels rise.

Get into bed wearing my coat after dinner.

16 FEBRUARY

Feeling slightly sick of marmalade, I return to the judging table after breakfast. But we rattle through them and decide on the winning jars, then I pack, say my goodbyes and return to the Penrith petrol station to pick up Dennis. He leaps all over me and we motor on to North Wales.

My godmother has refurbished a remote cottage near Snowdonia and offered it to me for a writing retreat. For almost two years, I've been researching and planning a book about a little-known Victorian heiress, and I'm going to spend the next two weeks away from the distractions of normal life in London, head down, immersed in Victoriana.

I get lost in the dark and take the wrong, narrow track, so reverse back down in the dark and eventually find the cottage up another long track and through a gate. Dennis bounds around, happily sniffing a new garden as I run a bath.

The Waitrose delivery man rings me an hour later saying he can't possibly get up the track to the cottage, so I drive down to meet him in my pyjamas and slippers, and ferry the shopping from his van into my car in the driving rain. Welcome to Wales.

17 FEBRUARY

I wake early, in a strange bed, and take Dennis to the nearest beach for a morning walk. It's wildly beautiful – acres of wet, flat sand, darkened by the retreating tide, and not another soul there. Dennis amuses himself by flinging pieces of seaweed into the air with his mouth and catching them as I watch the sun come up over the hills. I'm so lucky to be able to take myself (and Dennis) away to places so remote and extraordinary. I'll take the odd heartbreak so long as I can live a life like this.

18 FEBRUARY

Write a Substack headlined '40 things I know at (very nearly) 40.' Sometimes I feel as if I know less and less as I get older, but since I'm turning 40 tomorrow it seems as good a time as any to summarize the few things I have learned.

Always have a tissue in your pocket, I write. Never buy shoes that are too small in the mistaken belief that they'll stretch. Ditto jeans. You can never have too many lamps in a room. Initial your phone charger so family members can't 'borrow' it and later claim it's theirs. And so on.

Hardly Aristotelian. But useful all the same.

19 FEBRUARY

My birthday. I'm 40. I lie in bed and hold my hands in front of my face. They look the same to me.

Open a stack of cards I've brought from home, plus a few that have been sent to the cottage.

'You're going to be on your own, in Wales, on your *fortieth*?' various friends asked in advance, aghast, whereupon I told them I wouldn't be alone, because I'd have Dennis.

Actually, after the past eighteen months – falling in love, planning forever with Mike, getting Dennis, the break-up and realization that it was me and Dennis going forward – I wanted it to be just us today. A day of thinking about how far he and I have come in the past few months. A day of quiet celebration.

Rosie texts, 'What's Dennis given you?' I look at him, draped across my legs on the end of the bed, and think, 'Himself.'

Decide he and I can have the day off the Victorian novel and go for a walk. Turns out to be a more complicated route than I'd envisaged, involving bogs, barbed wire and a rickety bridge, which I carry Dennis over. At one point, I sink in mud so deep it comes up to my knees.

But during the trudging, I reflect. I'm now 40. No husband. No children. None of the usual signs of social success for a woman. But right then, legs sticky with mud, I'm genuinely, madly happy with my dog.

When we get back to the cottage, I bath him, then myself. Then the director calls for a tea-time video call. He's sitting at his dining table in Highgate, a pile of balloons behind him, then pans the camera to his kitchen, where there's a cake with candles. I have to 'blow' these out from Wales, behind my own computer screen, as he blows them out in London and cheers. It's such a generous, imaginative, creative thing to do that I'm quite dumbstruck for a moment. If he's doing this all for me, can he really be going on many other dates?

Later, I fry a steak for dinner, and eat while watching telly, Dennis asleep, pressed against my leg.

A properly wonderful birthday. Might make it just me and him every year.

20 FEBRUARY

Nearly (accidentally) kill Dennis again. We go for a walk along a river, fast-flowing because there's been so much rain recently, and he slips on the bank and falls in. 'Dennis! DENNIS!' I scream, feeling sick as I watch him wash away, but he manages to scrabble out a few metres down, then stands on the sodden bank, shivering.

I put him on the lead and follow the path to David Lloyd George's burial spot – surrounded by daffodils. Dennis has recovered sufficiently from the shock of nearly drowning to cock his leg on them.

Let him sleep on my bed, because he yelped throughout the previous night. I deliberately didn't bring a crate to Wales because I thought it could be the place where he transitions from crate to a proper dog bed. But he settled down on the duvet very happily tonight, like a husband who's been allowed back into the marital bed after some misdemeanour, so he clearly prefers my bed to his.

21 FEBRUARY

Not getting much of the Victorian novel done. Keep getting bogged down in the second chapter, when the 23-year-old Angela Burdett discovers that she's to inherit a vast fortune of millions, making her the richest woman in Europe. According to various accounts from the time, she was a tall, shy, plain woman with a severe hairstyle and a face marked with red blotches of eczema, but after that she was proposed to by every fortune hunter in the country. *Men*, I think wearily, as I rewrite the chapter because it doesn't feel dramatic enough.

Remind myself that it took Margaret Mitchell ten years to write *Gone with the Wind*. Epic historical masterpieces can't be written overnight, especially if the author has a small and demanding terrier to walk multiple times a day.

23 FEBRUARY

Nearly kill Dennis (yet again). A gloriously sunny day up here, so after writing until lunchtime, we set off for a long coastal walk. On a particularly deserted section, above Porth Neigwl beach, I scan and scan and scan again for sheep, then let him off the lead. Less than two minutes later, he races after a lone sheep. 'Dennis!' I scream, as he and the sheep tear towards the cliff edge and vanish over it.

The shock of it winds me and I burst into tears. 'Dennis!' I bleat. 'Dennis! Come back, Dennis!' I feel like a romantic heroine in a period drama, standing on a cliff edge, sobbing for her lost lover. I've killed my dog. I've thoughtlessly, stupidly killed my dog. Now I don't have a husband, children or Dennis. I have nothing, I'm alone, I'm an idiot. I deserve everything I get for being so careless and moron—

As I continue berating myself, I see movement to my right: a herd of sheep bustling towards me in the distance, a small white blur scurrying behind them. It's Dennis! The cliff wasn't a vertical cliff, just a very, very steep slope. He'd chased the sheep along it, underneath me, and was coming back around, having found the flock.

'DENNIS!' I scream. 'DENNIS!' I cannot recall ever having felt such a combination of relief and white-hot fury.

Flinging my rucksack to the ground, I pull out a small piece of cheese to coax him back.

'That is IT,' I said, grabbing him by the collar when he comes close. 'You're never going off the lead again. Ever. BAD DOG.'

His ears go back and he slinks quietly alongside me on his lead. The average dog apparently knows around 165 words, and I'm not convinced Dennis knew the exact words I was saying, but he certainly knew he was in trouble.

24 FEBRUARY

Go into the local bakery because I want to try an authentic Welsh cake. Realize, as I'm standing in the queue, that everyone around me is talking in Welsh – staff and customers. When I step up to the counter and say, 'Please could I have a Welsh cake?' I feel like the Queen. Are there any patches of Scotland or Ireland where the native language is still so widely spoken, or is it just Wales holding out?

Nearby, I also discover what must be the UK's best pet shop, with an entire wall of nose-to-tail dog treats, including pig snouts, rabbit ears, lamb trachea, turkey necks and ostrich feet.

'Very unprocessed,' I say approvingly to the assistant, as I buy a dried cow's nose and a toy dragon for Dennis.

'We did have a vegetarian come in once who turned green. We were a bit worried about her,' she tells me.

25 FEBRUARY

Bad writing day. I want the novel to be imbued with Victorian London – to smell and sound like Victorian London. But every line I write feels clichéd, like something from a teenage history essay.

Eat multiple pieces of shortbread in frustration. Go for walk. Come back. Watch Dennis play with his new dragon from behind my laptop – pouncing on it, then tossing it into the air, and catching it again with his mouth. Do I find this so entertaining because he's my dog? I could watch him for hours. He's become his own little person on this trip, scurrying around the garden, playing with his toys, chasing sea foam along the beach in the wind. On the passenger seat beside me today, he held his chew between his front paws, like a child with a lollipop, and seemed almost human.

In the past week or so, I've found myself watching him a lot, asleep on the carpet, legs in the air, or lying alongside my thigh on the sofa, and my heart has swelled. I've felt overwhelmed with love for this little creature who's become everything to me, and then I feel silly, sometimes, because he's just a dog, isn't he?

26 FEBRUARY

Have a sports massage thanks to a local masseur I found on Google. I've been writing so much in bed that my back is aching and stiff.

Tom the masseur lives in a big, cold farmhouse and spends half the year in Snowdonia, half in Thailand. He's extremely handsome and has enormous hands.

'Have you ever tried cupping?' he asks, a few minutes in.

I momentarily freeze under his enormous hands. Cupping. Is that a sex thing? Is he flirting? Is that a bit pervy when I'm lying on his massage bed? I've been in Wales for nearly two weeks with only a dog for company and seem to have lost the ability to interpret human words. Maybe I should flirt back? He is very handsome, but I don't know if I want to flirt with another man now, given that the director was so sweet on my birthday.

Fortunately, just as I'm trying to formulate an appropriate reply, Tom goes on to explain that cupping is a form of targeted massage, designed to ease specific tight spots. I lie on my front as he gets to work around my shoulder blades, placing small suction cups on my back. There's a tugging sensation on my skin for a minute or so on each spot, and then he takes the cup off. The idea, Tom explains, is to improve blood flow to that particular area. 'But you might have these marks for a couple of weeks,' he says nervously.

'That's alright, I'm not taking my clothes off in front of anyone up here,' I reply, before I can stop myself. Who's the pervert now, huh?

When Tom's finished and left the room, I stand up, look at my back in the mirror and gasp. It's pockmarked with big red circles, as if I've caught the plague. A good job the only man sharing my bed in Wales is Dennis, tbh.

27 FEBRUARY

Interview a Canadian writer via Zoom about her new memoir for *The Times*. The book's about divorce, because she split from her husband young, in her twenties. Not a very uplifting read, although there's a section where she writes about her and her husband trying an open marriage and reading a book called *The Ethical Slut* in preparation, which examines how to juggle open and polyamorous relationships.

'Have you heard of a book called *The Ethical Slut*?' I text the director.

'I've got it!' he replies.

Course he has.

I look it up on Amazon. 'Very old-fashioned,' says one review. 'Essentially a swingers' guide.'

Decide against buying a copy. Would feel self-conscious reading a book called *The Ethical Slut* on the Tube.

Take a photo of the red marks on my back and send it to the director. They've deepened in colour overnight. I look like I've been fondled by an octopus.

'Hot,' he replies. But then, he doesn't have great eyesight.

28 FEBRUARY

Spend my morning researching what Fortnum & Mason sold in the mid-Victorian age (turtle soup, game pies, candied fruits, marzipan), then take Dennis for another cliff walk.

Unfortunately, an hour or so in, he slipped the lead and scampered off into the gorse.

'Dennis!' I hissed, trying to avoid shouting because a couple were having a picnic lunch on a rock nearby.

Couldn't catch him for at least twenty minutes, which almost made me cry in fury, although the picnicking couple seemed to enjoy the spectacle. It wasn't until I sat and pulled out a piece of cake from my rucksack that he ventured close enough for me to grab his collar.

Funny how one can hate them, *really* hate them, in one moment, and then love them so furiously the next. I imagine it might be the same with children?

March

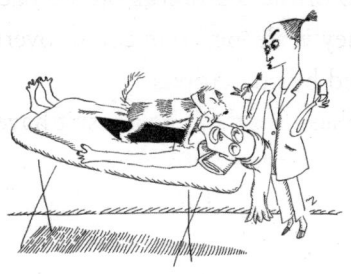

Things I googled in March:

- can you see fleas on dogs
- how to stop dog chasing chickens
- comfortable plimsolls
- how far can a one-year-old terrier walk
- pret prosciutto baguette calories
- what is retinol
- last woman to be hanged victorian britain
- the history of the crumpet
- what is a pikelet
- who invented the hot cross bun
- extra strength dog poo bags
- what jean shape fashionable now
- how to stop dog pulling lead
- tin foil which bin

1 MARCH

Walk up the hill behind the beach and sit with Dennis on a rock, overlooking the bay towards Anglesey. Our last walk. A glorious two weeks, give or take the odd sheep drama, although my Victorian novel remains very much a work in progress: six chapters down, roughly forty or so still to write.

I think back on holidays with ex-boyfriends. Or at least ex-lovers. The time I went to Greece with a war reporter who, on the last day, hobbled towards me on the beach, having stepped on a sea urchin, then thrust his foot under my nose and said I had to remove the spikes. The time I went to Sicily with another man, who refused to eat any seafood because he 'didn't trust it'. The time I went on a road trip from San Francisco to LA with an ex-boyfriend, and cried (in secret) every day because I'd realized that he and I weren't the right fit. The one who wanted to have sex every day, but only so that he could get himself off, never concerned about what I wanted. The ex who shouted at me for accidentally dropping my phone – *my* phone! – and smashing the screen, because he claimed it would be 'dangerous' if we got separated (we were in France).

Dennis, in the past two weeks, has done none of those things. Perhaps holidays with him are the way forward.

2 MARCH

The drive home from Wales takes seven and a half hours. Could have got to New York in less.

3 MARCH

The director texts early this morning, asking when we're next seeing one another. I'm desperate to see him, but reply saying that my week is crazy, having been away, and that I'm free next Monday.

'Catching up on your dating, clearly,' he texts back, which annoys me. He can't insist on being non-exclusive and quiz me like that, so I tell him that.

'It was unfair, sorry,' he replies instantly. 'My fault for not suggesting some dates earlier. Can I nab your Monday night slot and can we go to a nice restaurant somewhere?' he adds, which dissipates my bad temper.

By next Monday, we won't have seen each other for over a month, but whirlwinds haven't exactly worked out for me in the past. When it comes to dating, maybe it's better to be the tortoise than the hare?

4 MARCH

'Don't take this the wrong way,' said a woman in the park this morning, squinting at Dennis. 'But I used to have a stuffed dog on wheels that I pulled around behind me as a child, and your dog looks exactly like that.'

5 MARCH

Mum comes up to London for the night with Beano. He and Dennis race around in the garden together like small boys.

We go to an exhibition preview by the artist Gary Bunt at the Saatchi Gallery, where waiters are circulating with big flutes of champagne and silver trays of dainty canapés. Gary paints whimsical countryside scenes in oil, and they always feature a cartoonish old man and a small terrier. Mum and I love them, but I look at the price list and see they start at £9,500, so I buy a pack of ten postcards for a tenner. It makes me feel a bit like Hugh Grant in *Four Weddings and a Funeral*, when he can't afford anything on a wedding list, and the assistant jokes that he could buy several gift bags instead.

6 MARCH

Google 'dog trainer crystal palace' after a disastrous afternoon walk in the park in which Dennis refused to come back and leapt on a five-month-old spaniel puppy, causing the spaniel's owner to shriek loudly, 'Get off, get off!'

We need a star chart, I told him, as I wiped his paws when we got home, like people stick on the fridge for naughty toddlers. Today would be a no-stars day.

Dinner with two old schoolfriends in Soho. Lils announced she's pregnant, which is obviously wonderful, but I also felt a pang of self-pity. She's the very last of our schoolfriends to have children, apart from me. Everyone else will have them, and I may not. That does feel a bit lonely, sometimes.

7 MARCH

A message from the director this morning: 'Just checked. Five months ago today since we first said hello. Five months! See! I can be romantic!'

Chop up leftover pieces of broccoli and courgette and put them in Dennis's breakfast for vitamins and fibre, but he carefully eats around them, casting me accusing glances as he does. I laugh all morning at the sight of the ignored vegetables in his bowl. Maybe I don't need an actual toddler when I have one already.

8 MARCH

In Sussex for Mum's birthday weekend. She's turning 70 and throwing a small party. One of her best friends rushes up to me as soon as he arrives and says, 'I'm so sorry to hear about the boyfriend.'

'That's alright,' I reply, cheerfully, before explaining that I'm now in a non-exclusive relationship with someone else, and that I've accidentally embroiled myself in a very modern situation, 'a bit like couples who have open marriages or practise polyamory'.

He replies that he must get a drink and moves away quite quickly.

9 MARCH

My siblings and I take Mum for a celebratory birthday lunch at a local pub which has recently reopened after a £3m refurbishment. It's been in various papers as the hot new place for a minibreak, leading to inevitable cries that Sussex is 'the new Cotswolds'. I hope not. Sussex is quieter, less pretentious, and less full of Range Rovers than the Cotswolds.

I look around the table and think how magical it is that we've reached this landmark, given Mum's diagnosis eighteen months ago. A stage 4, metastasized brain tumour, and yet here we all are, happily eating roast beef.

'You're a medical marvel, Mother,' my brother tells her.

'Well, I am a bit,' says Mum.

Drive home and lie along the sofa watching Crufts, Dennis under my arm. He isn't one of those dogs who watches TV, which is a pity because a very fluffy Jack Russell called Ana makes it into the final, the first Jack Russell ever to reach the last round. Although she's beaten by an Italian whippet called Miuccia. Imagine standing in the park and shouting that.

10 MARCH

Ask Larry the Neighbour if he can dog-sit Dennis for the evening.

'Are you off to see that man?' he asks, eyes drawing together in suspicion. Larry is increasingly disapproving of the director. 'This simply isn't a relationship,' he shouted very loudly in the street last week, when I bumped into him on the way back from Sainsbury's.

The director and I don't go to a nice restaurant, like he suggested last week. Instead, I catch the Tube to Highgate because it's a Monday evening and both of us feel more like hanging on the sofa than going out.

First time seeing him in over a month, and as I sit in his kitchen and he cooks risotto, I can't help but think, 'Have you been dating in the past month? Have you slept with anyone else?'

We eat, sleep together, then I catch the Tube home again to pick up Dennis from Larry's, feeling ever so slightly like a sex worker.

11 MARCH

Take Dennis to a pub near Sloane Square for dinner with my friend Gem. There's another dog on the banquette seating at the table opposite us, so I let Dennis jump up and settle beside me on his blanket. Allowing dogs on restaurant seats is something I would have criticized a year ago.

Gem's dating a spy. At least I think she is. He works for the government, is being posted to Beijing in a year, and is currently undergoing intense Mandarin lessons. She's planning on moving to Beijing with him, but I can't help wondering whether leaving everything she knows, for a potential spy, is a good idea. We've all seen James Bond films.

I update her on the director and say I'm finding the non-exclusive rule increasingly confusing, because I like him but we're still in this weird place where we can date other people.

Might be easier dating a spy.

13 MARCH

Have a facial at a salon in Chelsea. Feel guilty about leaving Dennis at home, so ring the salon in advance and ask if I can bring my dog. 'He'll be very quiet and probably just sleep in the corner,' I promise. No problem, they tell me.

We arrive and are shown to a peaceful, dimly lit basement room with a large massage bed and the soft tweeting of birds playing through an overhead speaker. From my rucksack, I pull out Dennis's blanket and a chew, then tell him to settle down. I strip, lay back on the bed, and Shilpa the facialist comes back in.

Roughly three minutes after the facial begins, I hear the thud of paws on the side of the massage bed as Dennis tries to inspect what's going on. Moments later, he jumps up and I feel four paws trample all over my stomach, and his nose over mine, as he sniffs the cream that Shilpa was smoothing across my cheeks.

'Are you a dog person?' I ask her nervously.

Shilpa replies that she's a cat person, which feels like a more sensible life choice at that precise moment.

Dennis remained on the bed for the rest of my facial, shuffling around like a restless toddler. One moment he was lying by my side, the next he was draped across me like a draught excluder. I've had more relaxing hygienist appointments.

14 MARCH

There's a story in the *Evening Standard* today, headlined 'Woman eaten by pet sausage dogs as she lay dead in her home.' Poor woman apparently lay there for a month. I can't believe that Dennis would do the same if I keeled over, but perhaps that's naïve. It presumably starts with a little nibble of an earlobe, and then they work their way down from there.

Later, I go to my friend Ed's fortieth birthday party at a restaurant in Marylebone. Lots of champagne. I sit next to an actor and tell him about my non-exclusive relationship over dinner. He's about to get married and is full of advice. 'Does he make you happy? That's all you need to know,' he asked.

I'm not sure people who are about to get married are impartial sources of relationship advice.

16 MARCH

Meet Eve and the boys for a Sunday morning walk in Dulwich Woods.

'On our way. ETA about 15 minutes,' she texts, as Dennis and I walk there. 'Pet peeve,' she adds, 'people texting 5 minutes before meeting saying they're 15 minutes away.'

She arrives with a vast bag of croissants, hands one out to each of us like Mary Poppins, and we walk through the woods while the boys run ahead with Dennis and scream with joy at various graffitied penises that have mysteriously appeared on various trees in the past few months.

'Wish I could get so excited at the sight of a penis,' says Eve.

17 MARCH

Dennis clambers all over my laptop this morning as I was writing in bed, telling me it was time for a walk. It makes me cry with laughter – he pushes his paw across my keyboard to try to stop me writing, and casts resentful looks at the screen. So human again, somehow.

I never knew how many times a day a dog could make you laugh – he crawls up the bed in the morning to say he wants to go to the park. He comes and drops a toy on my foot when I'm working to say he wants to play. He sits by the garden door and glances over his shoulder at me when he wants to be let out and holler at the neighbour's cat.

Although later, he also makes me nearly spontaneously combust with anger and humiliation, because he races around the park like a small tornado and refuses to come back when called.

'He's giving me PTSD,' says another dog walker, as we watch Dennis misbehave. The dog walker used to have Jack Russells but now has a very obedient spaniel called Oz.

I tell him I've booked a session with a dog trainer for later this week. 'So, next time you see us, we'll be perfect.'

The dog walker lets out a big belly laugh at that, which seems a bit rude.

18 MARCH

Six months ago today, Mike broke up with me. I sit on the
sofa in my kitchen, looking at the spring sunshine and Dennis
digging a hole in the flowerbeds, dirt flying into the air behind
him, and I feel … fine?

Agree to a date with an artist from Hinge called Ryan.
I don't really want to date anyone else, but if the director's
dating others, then shouldn't I be, too?

20 MARCH

Dennis and I meet Alberto, the Crystal Palace dog whisperer
who's promised he can sort our recall issue out in one session.
I was hopeful that this session wouldn't be too long because
Alberto had explained his pricing in advance – £75 for the first
hour, and then £1 a minute after that, like an old-fashioned,
heavy-breathing chat line.

We started in my kitchen, where Alberto retrieved a packet
of supermarket frankfurters from his rucksack and sliced them
into tiny pieces. He went through various exercises – sit, down,
stay, leave it, heel – before we graduated to the park, where we
worked on recall using his squeaky ball as bait.

He gives me a lot of homework. There's no magic pill for
recall, it seems. Dog training is slow and repetitive and a tiny
bit boring, and I need to work on all Dennis's behaviour to
improve general obedience. I promise myself that I'll be better,
a session of training every day.

Alberto is extremely chatty and keeps breaking off from
our lesson to tell me about how he used to be a writer too, but

all I can think is 'This is costing me £1 a minute, Alberto! I'm not interested in your blog!'

It was a three and a half hour session in the end, but he took off 20 minutes and charged me £190. As we walked back towards my flat, Alberto announced that his drug dealer used to live on my street.

21 MARCH

Go to see *Unicorn* in the West End, a new play about a married couple who open up their marriage, invite a young woman into it, and become a 'throuple'.

The play was awful, with clunky writing, and even boring at points despite the technically sexy subject material and a starry cast. Although there was one moment when Stephen Mangan's character discusses 'butt play', which caused my friend Emma and me to dissolve into silent, shaking giggles in our seats, because the 60-something man and his wife in front of us looked so disgusted.

Various reviews have said the play illustrates society's 'changing attitudes' towards relationships, but I'm not sure they've changed quite so much. The vast majority of us must still be more into monogamy than not, surely? There's plenty of talk about polyamory, and open marriages, and people on dating apps who say they're into ENM (ethical non-monogamy). A polycule! A throuple! A quad! All these new words for new kinds of relationships. But although I'm experimenting with non-exclusivity at the moment, I'm not sure how much any of this is really going on in practice.

The 60-something couple in front of me certainly didn't seem like they'd be into the idea of a throuple.

22 MARCH

Drive to Whitstable for the weekend with the director. Call Shaunagh on the way.

'Darling,' she cries down the line. 'I'm delighted to see that the director's been upgraded to boyfriend!'

'What?' I shout, nearly driving off the road.

'In your *Telegraph* column today, it says "my new boy-friend".'

I mentioned that I've recently been 'seeing' a man in the column, but *The Telegraph* have extrapolated from this that he's my new boyfriend and stuck that in the headline. Christ. What will he say if he sees it? Luckily, he's a left-wing theatre director, so he probably won't.

We arrive, go for a walk on the beach and have fish and chips for lunch, then come back and lie on his sofa watching telly. Then one of the most embarrassing moments of my life occurs.

I went upstairs to have a bath and went to the loo while it was running. Unfortunately, the loo handle broke when I tried to flush it, which meant the contents of the loo were stuck, floating there.

Well, I panicked. Using a handful of loo paper, I scooped my poo from the loo and threw it in the bathroom bin. (Brief thought here: I've become used to picking up after Dennis, but how was I in a situation where I was picking up after myself?)

Then I threw a few toothbrush mugs of water into the loo to clear the discoloured water, but it didn't help much.

At that point, I knew I had to go downstairs and admit what had happened. 'OK, don't laugh,' I said, standing in front of the director with my hands covering my eyes, 'but I've had a bit of a disaster.'

He was so cool about it. He laughed, then set about trying to fix the loo handle while I took the bathroom bin outside, knotted the bag very firmly and left it in a street bin.

'Will you ever sleep with me again?' I mumbled into his shoulder, on the sofa afterwards, once I'd washed my hands. Very sweetly, he said there was nothing he found unsexy about me, but he was definitely fibbing because he'd just watched me carry his bathroom bin into the street.

After that, for the first time ever, we decided to attempt sleeping in the same bedroom together, instead of me sneaking out. He's bought something called 'hostage tape', which you stick over your mouth to prevent snoring. I'd like to know who chose that brand name.

As we went to bed, he stuck a piece of the black tape over his mouth to show me and I burst out laughing. Quite a bonding evening. If we can survive a loo embarrassment and hostage tape, surely this is a relationship worth giving a go?

23 MARCH

I sneaked out of bed and tiptoed into the spare room at 4 a.m. because the hostage tape wasn't working, then got up a couple of hours later to make a cup of tea and read my book on the sofa.

The director came downstairs in his dressing gown at 8 a.m., grumpy that the tape didn't work. 'How will we ever stay in a hotel together?' he demanded.

I replied in that scenario we might have to get a family room – him in one room, me and Dennis in the other.

24 MARCH

Wake up early to drive back to London and leave a hidden note in his shoe: 'Sorry about the loo.'

He texts me later. 'Just stepping out for a walk and found your note. Nothing to be sorry about. You're clearly just a bit of a yanker.'

I shudder with shame all over again. Perhaps this sort of accident is why other people are married and I'm not.

25 MARCH

Dennis was sick four times on the bus this morning. A woman opposite offered me her pack of tissues and then shifted further away to the window seat as I tried to mop it all up.

Arrived at Brockwell Park for the walking date with Ryan, the artist from Hinge. Dennis continued being sick and having diarrhoea for the first thirty minutes of our date, which was terrible. Nice enough man, but he talked largely about himself and described the countryside as 'reactionary', which I pretended I understood but didn't. We sat on a cold park bench for half an hour with our coffees, then politely said our goodbyes.

'If you do fancy getting together again, let me know,' he texted later, so I replied, saying no as charmingly as I could.

Dennis fine as soon as the date was over. Maybe he was trying to get me out of it.

26 MARCH

Take Dennis to Sydenham Woods to go foraging for wild garlic to make pesto, and we find a big patch, but a Great Dane bounds up and pisses all over it before I can pick any. Decide on watercress pesto for dinner instead.

27 MARCH

Supposed to be going on another Hinge date with a round-faced Australian called Tom, but I cancel it last minute because I don't want to go, and I'm not sure Dennis does either.

28 MARCH

Drive to Sussex for the night. Before Mum's diagnosis, she had several chickens, which scratched for worms and laid eggs in a pen at the end of her garden, but had to give them away when she was ill because they were too much to look after.

Last week, delightedly, she bought another five from a neighbour, so the pen is full of clucking chickens again, and Mum has fresh eggs in the morning. She's named them after the *Pride and Prejudice* sisters.

Unfortunately, within a few minutes of letting Dennis out

of my car, he'd worked out how to wriggle under the fence and get into the pen. He cornered Lydia, the brown one, then cantered around the garden carrying her in his mouth while I screamed at him to put her down.

Eventually, he dropped her and she escaped into the neighbour's garden. I shut Dennis inside, then Mum and I tended to poor Lydia. She was shaken and had a bit of a limp, so we watched her for a while, but she didn't seem fatally wounded.

Dennis in disgrace but he didn't seem to know it. Played with Beano all evening, bouncing up and down on the sofa.

29 MARCH

Astonishingly, Lydia laid an egg overnight.

'I'm not surprised,' said Mum, coming in from the hen house. 'I'd probably lay an egg after that ordeal.'

We drive to Kent for a session of sheep training. After the sheep dramas in Wales, various people recommended a farmer called Tobin, who runs a business called Sheep Proof Your Dog. Mum came too because she said Beano could do with a spell of training on that front.

I took Dennis first, on a lead, into a small pen with three sheep. If he lunged at them, Tobin screamed 'No!' at him louder than I've ever heard anyone scream before, while also rattling two empty Coke bottles – filled with an inch of small stones – at his head. They were like very aggressive maracas.

We progressed from the pen to a small field where the same process happened, then an even bigger field, by which point

Dennis and Beano seemed to have got the message: chasing or even looking at sheep was *bad*.

'If you don't mind me saying,' Tobin says, at the end of our session, frowning down at Dennis, 'he could probably do with a bit more discipline at home.'

I ask whether his training method would also work with chickens. Yes, says Tobin, it should work with anything I don't want him to chase.

Make a mental note to fashion my own Coke-bottle maraca when I get home.

30 MARCH

The clocks have gone forward and it's a gloriously sunny Sunday. Take Dennis north to Hampstead for a walk on the heath, then to the director's house because we're having lunch with his friends. One of them refers to me as his girlfriend, so I glance across the table to see if he's panicked, but he gives me a reassuring smile.

Another of the friends has a spaniel the same age as Dennis, so we take them to the park after lunch and laugh as they race around together in circles, playing. 'If you want to meet someone, get a dog,' people often say, and I've doubted this from time to time over the past few months. But maybe they can help in dating situations.

Well done, Dennis, I think, as the director squeezes my hand.

April

Things I googled in April:

- why do dogs hide bones
- how long is too long for a voice note
- did victorian women wear knickers
- is my dog tax deductible
- half sweet potato calories
- how much does a human head weigh
- 15000 steps a day how many calories
- can kefir make you constipated
- world custard pie championship
- did ted bundy have children
- if you have a dog how likely is it that you get worms
- best earplugs for snoring
- bromley garden waste collection day

1 APRIL

Go and see Ben Fogle on stage in Bromley. We've been friends since I interviewed him and his wife Marina some years ago for *Tatler*. Come to the show early and say hi, Ben told me.

I knock on the stage door and weave my way around the backstage warren to find him. He's been thinking about a podcast, he says, and we discuss making a podcast about dogs. I worry slightly that certain sections of the internet might be upset at the idea of two posh white people talking about their Labradors (which Ben has) and a terrier (Dennis). It feels like the sort of project that some might genuinely assume was an April Fool.

2 APRIL

Dash! I'm so relieved to see him on our walk home from the park that I cry his name aloud. Dennis is also pretty excited, straining on the lead like a pitbull, little front legs scrabbling to get closer to him.

'No!' I shout, deciding to put some of Tobin's training into practice.

Dennis, surprised by this sudden attempt at discipline, crouches down low on the pavement, ears back, tail tucked behind his legs. His eyes look up at me fearfully, uncertain what he's done wrong.

Oh God, the guilt. I squat down and reassure him with a few strokes. 'Come on, puppy dog, let's go and have breakfast,'

I say, knowing that the 'b' word will cheer him up again. So that was my sole attempt at discipline.

Dash watches all this from across the road, unbothered, his tail swishing from side to side.

3 APRIL

A sunny afternoon in the park – picnics, small toddlers waddling about on the grass, an ice-cream van, and dog walkers taking advantage of the dappled shade in the woods.

Dennis and I potter around slowly in the heat and pass a man the size of Hagrid standing very still, with an enormous camera lens trained on a branch overhead.

Dennis pauses to sniff his boot, and before I can stop him, cocks his leg and starts piddling all over the birdspotter's shin.

'Dennis, no!' I shout, but too late.

The man drops his camera lens and looks at his leg in horror. 'What the hell?'

'I'm so sorry, I'm so sorry, I don't have any tissues, I'm so sorry,' I gabble, as the birder blinks down at his leg, glares at me, glares at Dennis, then blinks again at his leg.

Dennis, unrepentant, trots on ahead.

'I'm so sorry,' I repeat. 'Can I … er … give you this?' I pull a poo bag from my pocket.

'That's not going to do much good, is it?' he snarls, and I have to admit that, no, a plastic poo bag probably wasn't going to be much use on a damp leg.

We walk on in different directions: me, cringing with

embarrassment; the birder, furious; Dennis, oblivious, finishing a child's dropped ice-cream nearby.

He must have thought the birder's leg was a tree trunk because it was so sturdy. We would have done another lap, but I didn't want to risk bumping into the same man again, so I bundle Dennis into the car and tell him we have to go home.

4 APRIL

Larry the Neighbour baby-sits Dennis for the evening so I can drive to Braintree, where I'm interviewing a new musical star. ('At least you're not seeing that man,' Larry says cheerfully, as I hand Dennis over.)

James Partridge has performed to sold-out audiences across the country and at Glastonbury in the past year, but his material is quite unusual: assembly songs. He plays his keyboard and sings songs like 'He's Got the Whole World in His Hands' and 'One More Step Along the World I Go' to 30- and 40-somethings who remember them from school. It's a different Friday night, queueing in an Essex venue for a white wine before sitting down to a giant singalong, but surprisingly enjoyable. I sit next to a primary school teacher who's come with her two daughters, who've smuggled wine in a box in with them. On my other side is Jo, a police officer on a night off. Luckily, she doesn't notice the contraband wine.

5 APRIL

Drive to Highgate to spend the night with the director. It's still warm at 5 p.m., so we take Dennis for a stroll in the woods. I tell him I'm going to a wedding next weekend, and he quips back, 'Maybe you'll meet someone,' which stings at first, then makes me sad, then angry. I've just driven across London to see him, and bought dinner because he said he didn't know what to cook. Why am I even bothering with this? With him?

I don't say anything, because I've never been one of those people who can confront something hurtful at the time it's said, but I mull it over for the rest of the evening.

6 APRIL

Break up with the director. Or try to, anyway. Send him a voice note, tearily explaining that I think we have to go separate ways, that he and I want different things. I'm not sure breaking up with someone in a voice note is good etiquette (is it?), but I want to put across my side without him interrupting, to explain why I'm doing this without getting muddled.

Then I lie on my bed, pretending to read, my phone lying beside me so I can see when the screen lights up with a reply.

He calls instead, and we talk for nearly two hours.

'What do you want?' he asks. 'Because you never actually tell me, by the way.'

I've always assumed, I reply, that this could only be a casual relationship because he's been clear that he doesn't do exclusivity. But I like him more than that now, I add, so the situation's become too confusing.

He suggests that we go away together for a week, to properly hang out and spend time together, and see whether we want to do this properly after that. Spain, we decide. I have a week booked at my dad's house, while he's away, so we'll go there together in June. A relaxed, chilled, very low-stakes holiday, I joke.

The strongest, best couples I know didn't seem to have any confusion from the start; it was as if they simply recognized one another after a lifetime apart. But I also know you don't find whatever this is every day on Hinge. So, let's see.

Spain. No pressure.

7 APRIL

'How are you today?' the director texts.

Better, I tell him. And relieved, and I say I'm going to send flight details for our make-or-break holiday.

'I'm so glad you're happier,' he texts back. 'Me too, actually. Like Bob Hoskins said, it's good to talk. You're too young to get that.'

'I do know who he is,' I reply. 'He's the one who sang "Mr Tambourine Man".'

'I sincerely hope that's a joke,' he answers.

I laugh to myself as I type that it is, and feel a welcome wave of relief that we're back to silly text messages again. Back to us.

Later, watching TV, I notice Dennis licking the same spot

on his paw, over and over. He won't let me inspect it, snapping at me like a lion cub as I try, but eventually I see a cut behind his dew claw. It's not bleeding, but deep. In a panic, I ring the emergency vet. If it's not bleeding, she says, cover it overnight and bring him in the next day.

I hurry to Sainsbury's to buy some gauze and medical tape. But when I get back, without anyone else to help, there's simply no way I can wrap it around his leg. Dennis keeps snarling and growling when I try, then retreating behind the sofa to lick it again.

I let him sleep on my bed as compensation. 'Please can you stop licking it? Dennis, poppet, please stop it,' I tell him.

He settles against my leg with a heavy sigh, then continues to lick the cut.

8 APRIL

The vet was traumatic (for us both). Dennis wouldn't let Martin near his leg, so I had to help muzzle him, but he wriggled so violently that he slipped that off, too.

'Do you think he'll be better if you're not here?' Martin asks. 'Otherwise we might have to sedate him so I can get a proper look.'

He takes him to another room downstairs while I hover anxiously in reception, wondering how much sedation will cost.

Ten minutes later, Martin returns with a perfectly bouncy Dennis.

'It's better than I thought,' he says. 'A cut, but already healing pretty well.'

He tells me to monitor it over the next few days, prescribes Dennis a bottle of what is essentially dog Calpol, and I settle a bill for £104.

Driving home, I listen to a news story on the radio, revealing that scientists have discovered that having a dog or cat can boost its owner's wellbeing more than a partner. In times of stress, our pets are supposedly more of a comfort than our other half.

I'm not sure they're necessarily more of a comfort *every* day, I think, as I watch Dennis race into the garden when we get back from our expensive outing, his paw mysteriously improved.

9 APRIL

Happy birthday, Dennis. One today. Babies at this age should be able to sit independently, pull themselves up and maybe even take a few steps.

Dennis can sit (when bribed with a biscuit). He's good at steps, and very adept at jumping up and down on my bed, often leaving little paw prints on the sheets if he's just come in from the garden. He isn't a fussy eater, he's (mostly) potty trained, and he sleeps through the night. Unfortunately, he still likes tugging my knickers out of the laundry basket, and he won't necessarily come back if I shout his name in the park. But still, pretty good, I reckon. Pretty great, in fact. I'm so grateful he's here.

The WhatsApp group of his siblings, created by Lorraine the breeder when we all picked up our puppies last summer, bursts into life with celebratory pictures of Dennis's brothers and sisters – a snap of Bob on his morning walk in Scotland, of Cece scampering about her garden, and Bear on the sofa at home in Warwickshire. I send one of Dennis lying on my bed, looking at me expectantly. 'Happy birthday from Dennis!' I write. 'He's making the face that means it's time to go to the park.'

That afternoon, we go to the posh Dulwich butcher on the way back from our walk and I buy him a big marrow bone for his birthday tea. He spends the next few hours eating it in the garden, dragging it from spot to spot on the grass. After that, he has quite bad diarrhoea. Like a small child who's had too much birthday cake.

10 APRIL

Sam, my editor at *You* magazine, emails asking if I can interview Jilly Cooper later this month, to celebrate the fortieth anniversary of her first bonkbuster, *Riders*. Have never replied to an email faster. 'Yes PLEASE,' I write back.

In 2018, when my first novel came out, Jilly gave me a brilliant quote for the front cover – 'the sex makes me feel like a nun'. I sent her a case of champagne as a thank you, and we've chatted on the phone a few times since, but never actually met. Now I'm going to her house in the Cotswolds for the day. This feels even more thrilling than flying to New York to interview Brooke Shields.

'Can I take Dennis?' I ask Sam, and he says he'll check with Jilly's PA. Later, he replies saying she wants to know what kind of dog Dennis is.

'A parson terrier,' I tell him, hoping that Jilly will approve.

11 APRIL

There's a story in *The Times* today about the boom in 'puppy Prozac' because the number of British dogs taking the anti-depressant in the past decade has increased tenfold. Vets are blaming Covid for creating anxious dogs that were cooped up, but also over-nannying owners who want their dogs to be 'fur babies'.

Some years ago, very low after another break-up, I went to see my GP, explained my symptoms (weeping, exhaustion, general bleakness), whereupon she immediately asked whether I'd considered antidepressants.

I shook my head, uncertain that they were the answer, and within a few months, my heartbreak had eased.

I've wondered many times over the past few months whether Dennis has acted as a natural antidepressant. 'That puppy will help,' Shaunagh told me in September, after Mike left, 'because you'll have to put one foot in front of the other.'

But it's been about more than just walking and feeding him. It's been about talking to him, playing with him, dancing in front of him when Fleetwood Mac comes on the radio (poor Dennis), wandering about naked in front of him, being totally unselfconscious and wholly *me* with him. We spend our lives trying to be perfect partners, parents, children, siblings, friends, colleagues, but there's no trying with a dog. With Dennis, I can be completely myself, an enormous relief after years of trying to be a better writer, to be skinnier, to eat less, read more, take more exercise, drink less. Dennis doesn't need me to be better in any way. He just needs me to be me.

'Anyone who calls their dog a fur baby should be automatically banned from having one,' says a comment underneath the *Times* article. I don't disagree.

14 APRIL

Go to the Young Vic with the director. It's the first time we've seen one another since the big conversation. He's booked his flights for Spain, he says, and I feel a spike of happiness that we're going to have proper time together.

We watch the play and have a drink in the bar afterwards, and I meet a friend of his who played the lead role. It feels oddly normal for a fairly abnormal relationship, but then I go home to South London afterwards and he goes back to North London. No staying with one another during the week on account of Dennis – and the director's snoring.

Luckily, there are three bedrooms in Spain, I text him on the Tube.

15 APRIL

Larry the Neighbour knocked on my door around 6 p.m. this evening. 'Does Dennis want to come for a walk?'

I was exhausted after a long day of trying to write a proposal scene between the Victorian heiress and her much older lover, but I knew Dennis would be delighted, so put him on the lead and hand him over, along with his favourite ball.

An hour later, my phone rings. It's Larry, hysterical. 'You're going to have to come and get him. He won't come back! He's uncontrollable!'

'Have you tried bribing him with the ball?'

'The ball? THE BALL? Oh, we lost the ball *days* ago. Take it up with your dog!'

Wearily, I pull my trainers on and walk to the park to find them. See Larry coming towards me through the trees, with Dennis trotting happily on the lead behind him.

'It took three of us to catch him,' he shrieks. 'I've done 15,000 steps!'

As we walk back, he interrogates me about the director, so I tell him we're going away together in a month to decide.

'Perhaps that's why Dennis is acting up,' Larry suggests. 'Poor baby has such a terribly unstable home life.'

16 APRIL

First outside dinner of the year, at a trendy wine bar in Herne Hill with Eve, packed tables all around us, people smoking and drinking rosé. It feels like the whole city is celebrating the fact we can now risk sitting outdoors without coats on. Dennis lies on his blanket underneath my chair, distracted by a pizzle stick. The revolting smell is wafting upwards, which I hope isn't off-putting for the couple beside us, clearly on a date.

'What's happening with you guys getting a dog?' I ask Eve.

She flutters her lips like a horse. 'Not happening, not at the moment. Jake sent me a link last week to an article claiming that dogs help children's cognitive development, and then I found Charlie in the garden having just eaten half a worm, so he's probably a lost cause anyway. But we've got too much on our hands, and I'll be the one who ends up having to do all the work.'

Why only half the worm, I ask, and Eve replies that Charlie had saved the other half for her.

It is a lot, I tell her, to be comforting. I think back to the 3 a.m. trips to the garden, and the 5 a.m. starts, and the endless wet patches on the carpets, and the moments I wondered if I should send Dennis back, and then I drop my hand underneath my chair to check he's still there.

17 APRIL

'Have you given your dog drugs?' asks Jeremy Vine from the radio while I'm writing at my kitchen table and Dennis is in the garden, throwing one of my socks in the air with his mouth and trying to catch it.

Apparently, a Jack Russell puppy from Burnley ate a bag of cannabis he found on a walk in the park, leaving its owner with a £500 vet bill, so they're covering the subject on Radio 2.

Jeremy interviews a man called Darren, whose dog once ate a bag of marijuana.

'Did it survive?' he asks.

'Yes, it fell asleep for, ooooh, roughly two and a half days,' Darren replies cheerfully.

'OK, thank you, Darren,' Jeremy says briskly, before moving on to another caller. 'Now your dog ate cocaine, how was *that*?'

'That's not quite accurate,' says the caller. 'It wasn't a dog. It was a meerkat.'

'Goodness gracious me,' says Jeremy. 'How much cocaine?'

'Well, meerkats don't need a lot,' the caller replies.

18 APRIL

Drive to my stepsister Elizabeth's house in Kent for the weekend, praying that Dennis won't jump on the sofas, jump on anyone's legs, go upstairs, pee on the carpet, do a poo anywhere inside, or be too boisterous with their elderly spaniel, Noodle.

We arrive and he immediately leaps from the car and pounces all over Noodle as if she's his long-lost relative.

20 APRIL

Easter Sunday. Leave Kent after a big lunch of garlicky roast lamb and get in the car to go and see the director.

Unfortunately, there's a crash on the M25, and Dennis and I sit in standstill traffic for two hours while I try to ignore how badly I need to pee.

After one hour, I can't ignore it any longer, reach for Dennis's water bottle in the back, tug my jeans down as subtly as I can in the driver's seat and relieve myself into the bottle.

If anyone glances over from one of the standstill cars around me, they'll either know what I'm doing, or think I'm fiddling with my crotch for a different reason.

'I'm so sorry, Dennis, I'll get you another one,' I tell him, as I fling the warm bottle into the footwell.

Eventually, accident cleared, I arrive at the director's house stinking of garlic and, quite possibly, pee. I broke his loo in Whitstable and now this. But when I tell him he just laughs and hugs me, then runs me a bath.

21 APRIL

Bank holiday Monday. Go to garden centre with director. Buy a tree for his garden and an orchid for me. 'Extremely middle-class couple behaviour,' I warn him, as we drive home, Dennis sandwiched between the potted plants in the back.

23 APRIL

Go to a friend's book launch in Dulwich and meet the man who created *Casualty*. He met our mutual friend, the author, on a dog walk in Brockwell Park, so we discuss dogs for some time. Did I know that there was a big dog cull in Britain just before the Second World War, he asks me. Worried about a Nazi invasion and how they were going to feed their pets during war, hundreds of thousands of British pet owners apparently had their dogs put down.

'How about that for a TV drama?' I say brightly, trying to impress this important TV man.

He gives me an incredulous look.

No, OK. I suppose a TV drama about the massacre of 750,000 dogs (and cats) probably wouldn't be a very cheerful watch.

24 APRIL

A day volunteering at the Marsden. Dennis goes to Noah's Bark, the doggy daycare centre. At lunchtime, I get a video of him, set to music, playing on the trampoline with a dog called Dexter. If I ever feel guilty about leaving Dennis at home in the evening when I go out, I'm going to watch this video back and remember that he has a more pampered life than a royal child.

25 APRIL

Drive to Norfolk for the weekend to stay with my friend Fi, a TV producer I met years ago when I filmed a TV segment on 'the etiquette of the threesome'. I'd recently written a very tongue-in-cheek piece for *Tatler* on the subject. Fi was making a late-night show for Channel 4 on the country's top ten fetishes, and because she's charming and funny and immensely flattering, she got me on national television – in my best boarding-school accent – talking about threesomes. That was how we became friends.

She lives in an idyllic, remote cottage surrounded by woods, with a stream close by, and her two pointers, Moby and Mits. Dennis is in heaven – two bigger dogs to play with, and a vast garden to do it in.

Fi's tall artist friend Ben also arrives for the weekend, and sets about putting up his tent in the garden, since I'm in the only spare room. I've met him once before and was struck by his handsomeness.

'Could you and he maybe ...' Fi suggests, as we watch Ben drive his tent pegs into the ground.

'It's complicated,' I say, and begin telling her about the director.

26 APRIL

Ben, Fi and I go to a nearby market and I squeal with excitement when I see several crates of British asparagus – fat green stalks as thick as an index finger.

The vegetable man tells us proudly that he supplies Waitrose with asparagus, but these are the stems they've rejected for being too wonky. They don't look wonky to me. They look perfect, so I buy four big bunches.

So hot this afternoon that all the dogs swim in the stream and chase one another around the garden. Makes me wonder whether I should move to the country. But I cannot possibly make that sort of major life decision on the basis that a bigger garden would be nicer for Dennis. People move to the country so their children can go to better schools and breathe clean air. Not sure I can do the same for a dog, can I? But he isn't just a dog to me now. He's become so much more.

27 APRIL

Dennis's first boat trip. Ben and I carry Fi's dusty kayak through the woods, and over great clumps of nettles, then drop it in the water and float back downstream. Dennis stands behind me, front paws on the side, like a ship dog looking over my shoulder for pirates.

Later, I drive across the country from Norfolk to the Cotswolds, where I've booked a dog-friendly hotel for two nights before my interview with Jilly Cooper, who lives nearby.

In the room, they've left dog treats, poo bags, a dog bed, a dog bowl, and a polite notice asking that dogs stay off the bed. Dennis immediately jumps on the bed with one of the chews.

I do some Jilly research in front of *Antiques Roadshow*, while Dennis spends all evening hiding his chew behind the pillows before retrieving it again. He's only started hiding bones or chews recently. According to Google, it's an ancient instinct, dating from when dogs needed to hide resources and save them for later.

I suspect Dennis is safe from starvation in a Cotswold hotel, given that he has two solid meals a day and roughly sixty-three snacks in between, but you never can be too careful.

28 APRIL

Spend all day researching Jilly. My editor has sent me a very comprehensive brief – can I ask her about her husbands' affairs? Can I ask her about how much sex she had as a young wife? Can I ask her about whether she feels she's been a bad mother?

I feel uncomfortable about quizzing an 88-year-old woman on her late husband's sex life, as well as her own, but this is also the author who wrote of one character plunging into his lover 'as joyously as an otter diving into a summer stream', so perhaps she won't mind? Be more Jeremy Paxman, I tell myself. Don't be such a wimp.

Research finished, Dennis and I go for dinner with my friend Netia, who lives in a very beautiful house not far from the hotel – all yellow Cotswolds stone and lilac wisteria hanging over the kitchen door.

Netia has four terriers, so they and Dennis race around the garden while we have a glass of rosé in the evening sun. But, very suddenly, as if stung by a bee, she leaps up from her chair. 'He's fallen in,' she says, before tearing through the garden towards the pond.

Dennis is scrabbling in the water, unable to climb out because the walls of the raised pond are too high. Netia hoiks him out by his collar, and he stands dripping on the grass, little stomach heaving in and out for breath. She'd heard the splash and I hadn't.

Thank God she heard it, I think, crouching by a wet Dennis. Otherwise, he could have been scrabbling in the water for ages before we realized what had happened. Or drowned. The thought makes me feel sick, so I pour us another glass of rosé and let Dennis, wrapped in a towel, sit on my lap like a damp, pink-cheeked baby after a bath.

29 APRIL

Jilly was standing in her drive when I arrived, frail and on a stick, wearing a jersey with a terrier on it. Her assistant asked what breed he was in advance, and Jilly has – incredibly sweetly – dressed accordingly.

'Hello, darling,' she says, as if we're old friends, before we go inside and Amanda, the assistant, makes us coffee. Turns out Dennis is quite a good icebreaker, because we discuss him for several minutes before getting down to the interview.

Everyone was having sex all the time, back in the day, says Jilly, who seems enormously keen to discuss her favourite subject. Sean Connery and his wife came for dinner in the 1970s, she adds, and he kissed Jilly in her kitchen. They were both married. 'But then he called me up the next day and said we probably shouldn't have an affair,' she tells me. 'Wasn't that sweet?'

'Quite sweet,' I venture, 'but if one of my girlfriends snogged another man in the kitchen, I think their husband might be quite upset.'

'Would they really?' Jilly replies, shocked. The odd 'necking' or 'bonk' simply wasn't a big deal in her day, she insists.

This leads her to ask about my own love life. I sigh and explain that I'm in a non-exclusive situation with a theatre director.

Jilly tuts. 'Where are the decent men? They can't *all* be gay.'

Dennis farts at one stage, which I only mention in case Jilly thinks it's me. 'That doesn't matter a bit, does it, darling?' she tells Dennis, clutching him. 'You can do whatever you want.'

30 APRIL

Dinner with three girlfriends in Soho. They all have several children, aged between a few months and seven years old. I mention Dennis a couple of times, before one of them starts talking about how tricky her one-year-old son's being at night. 'Sorry,' she says after a few moments of discussion on the subject, looking at me, 'but we did let you do *quite* a lot of dog chat.'

In a heartbeat, I feel silly. I have Dennis; they have children. I know that children are more significant than dogs. I don't want to be one of those women who becomes so obsessed with Dennis that I consider him a child. But I still feel that sinking playground feeling of being left out, diminished, smaller in some way.

May

Things I googled in May:

- 1 banana calories
- dog being bit manic after chicken bone
- how many people have been killed by a penny farthing
- can you die from overeating asparagus
- how many dogs get blown off cliffs a year
- what does the handshake emoji mean
- best squeaky balls amazon
- how long is too long for a voice note
- swimsuit for long bodies
- find it hard to work with pmt
- dirty martini calories
- plural of octopus
- male celebrities in espadrilles
- bromley bin collection today blue bins

1 MAY

Take Dennis to the groomer for his summer haircut. When I return to pick him up a couple of hours later, I glance through the window at the table where he's being dusted off, like a barber tidies a client's shoulders after a trim. I laugh and Dennis immediately looks up, and his tail goes wild with excitement. My heart leaps.

2 MAY

Bank holiday weekend. Dennis and I drive to Whitstable for three days with the director. Stop at a farm shop on the way down because I saw a big 'ASPARAGUS' sign outside it.

Inside, I find a chatty woman sifting through crates of asparagus from the farm, so I buy a giant bundle, plus some goose eggs and apple juice.

'Have you got any more eggs?' I ask.

'I'll just go and see if they've laid,' she replies, and nips out the back.

While waiting, I notice they have two parson terriers. One's called Russell, the lady tells me when she returns with the eggs, and the other's called Fluff, who's 18 and apparently had a stroke the previous day, although he seems perfectly perky to me.

Her husband, the farmer, makes me go and retrieve Dennis from the car so he and his wife can inspect him, whereupon Russell becomes over-excited at the sight of Dennis, and Dennis becomes over-excited at the sight of the geese, so I have to quite quickly put him back in the car again.

The director, Dennis and I stroll along the sea front and drink half-pints of cider while watching the sun set, then walk back to his house for goose-egg omelette and asparagus, almost like a couple.

3 MAY

Sunshine. A walk. Oysters. More cider. Back to the house for the Arsenal game, and I fall asleep with my head on the director's chest while we watch a quiz show.

4 MAY

A day trip to Margate to see an exhibition at the Turner, then lunch in a posh restaurant overlooking the sea. Something about the effort the director's gone to makes me want to cry – he's determinedly avoided relationships for years, but this feels like he's tentatively trying to be like everyone else, he's trying something that a couple might do. It makes me think of E.T. putting on his blonde wig and trying to be more human (I don't share this thought about E.T. with him). We drive back to Whitstable, walk Dennis along the shingle, then lie entangled on his sofa. I've had such a happy weekend I don't even mind that he makes us watch the World Snooker Championships.

5 MAY

I have that sinking feeling about leaving Whitstable. The director and I have such long gaps between seeing one another – will it be one week? Two weeks? Three weeks? More?

He sends me a sweet voice note that evening, when we're both home in opposite ends of London, saying how much he enjoyed the weekend and how much he's looking forward to Spain or, as I've dubbed it, 'our decider holiday'.

I'm looking forward to it too, even though I'm uncertain of what I want myself.

6 MAY

Take Dennis to a work pub quiz. The psychotherapist Philippa Perry is sitting behind me on a different team, and we end up discussing whether or not I should have a baby. 'Oh, go on, just have a baby,' she tells me, as if I'm deciding whether or not to have something from the pudding menu.

7 MAY

Go to my stepbrother Harry's house to see his new baby, Max.

'Would I want this?' I wonder, as I hold him and look down at Max's tiny, puckered mouth. 'Would I want one if I was doing it by myself?'

I'm not sure I could afford to do it by myself. I read recently that, in Hungary, if you're a woman with over three children, you're forever exempt from paying income tax. Maybe I should move to Budapest.

Dennis jumps up, desperate to see the small bundle in my arms, so he's keen, anyway.

9 MAY

When I arrive at Mum's for the weekend, the old lawn mower is strapped to the gate of the chicken pen with a bungee. 'Safety measure,' she explains. 'To make sure Dennis doesn't wriggle underneath.'

It doesn't stop him from sitting on the doorstep, looking longingly beyond the lawn mower at Jane, Lizzy, Mary, Kitty and Lydia, who carry on scratching for earwigs until dusk.

10 MAY

So hot the air shimmers above the Sussex fields. Take Dennis and Beano to the stream for a swim. Dennis thinks the calves in the field are big dogs and keeps bounding up to them until I summon him away with a biscuit. I check the statistics later – apparently four to five dog walkers are killed every year by stampeding cows.

According to one report, women are more likely to protect their dogs, whereas men will let them go, which is the recommended advice. If a herd of cattle was galloping towards me, I'm pretty sure I'd let Dennis go and run for it separately. Surely it's every man for himself, by that point.

12 MAY

Go to the open-air theatre in Regent's Park with the director to see a musical that's transferred from Broadway. Just before the interval, the sky turns a deep pink and a brace of ducks fly overhead and quack, which you never get in a cramped West End theatre.

'Pretty romantic, huh?' the director says, coming back to our seats with two ice-creams. It is, I agree.

He also remarks, not accusingly, but maybe wistfully, that if I didn't have Dennis at home I could come back to his flat in Highgate. That's true, but the idea that he could come back to mine didn't seem to occur to him. This seems to be the trouble with dating when you're that much older: both parties are more stuck in their ways, and neither wants to give up sleeping in their own bed.

Pick Dennis up from Larry the Neighbour just before midnight. 'How was it?' he asks suspiciously.

'Nice,' I tell him.

'Nice!' Larry says with scorn. 'You can't be with him just because you want to be with *someone*.'

I'm not sure that's what I'm doing, I think, as I walk Dennis home. He was just someone months ago. Just someone I happened to meet on a dating app. Just someone who was a distraction after Mike left. But he's not just someone anymore. It hasn't been straightforward but I have come to love him. I love him for his openness and his unconventionality, for his talent and his teasing sense of humour. I love him for the way he's never fazed by anything, and his calmness when it comes to dealing with dramas like a broken loo. I love him for his generosity and for his kindness, for the methodical way he puts chocolate and sweets in a bowl for us to have on the sofa after dinner. I love him for the stupid face he pulls in selfies and even for his absurdly long voice notes.

But I still don't know if I love him enough. And then I think: what is enough?

15 MAY

Mum rings and sounds sad. Beano has killed two Bennet sisters – Kitty and Lydia. She let them out of the chicken pen into the wider garden for a change of scenery, and although Beano's more trained than Dennis, unfortunately they wandered into the kitchen and he went for them. 'He was perfectly happy hanging out with them in the garden,' she says, 'but when they crossed the threshold of the house he turned into Bluebeard.'

This makes me feel a tiny bit smug about Dennis. Chicken tally: Beano – 2, Dennis – 0.

17 MAY

Exactly a year ago, I drove three hours north to meet a five-week-old puppy, having seen photos of him online. He was so small I could hold him in my palm, and I texted Mike excitedly as I left, saying that I'd found the one, I'd found our puppy.

I wouldn't take any of it back. Without Mike, I'd never have found Dennis. Without Dennis, my life would be very different. Cheaper and less embarrassing. I wouldn't be on first name terms with Martin the vet. I wouldn't find biscuit crumbs and poo bags in every pocket. My bedroom carpet wouldn't be stained from accidents when he was small, and the kitchen floor wouldn't be covered with disembowelled toys, chews and tennis balls.

But life would be so much less joyful. Lonelier. I'd miss Dennis's weight against my foot when I have a cup of tea in bed in the morning. I'd miss the desperately mournful face he makes when he wants to go to the park. I'd miss watching him patrol for squirrels in the garden. I'd miss his jaunty canter, and the dramatic little sigh he makes every time he flops down on the sofa, as if he has the hardest life of anyone he knows. I'd miss the way he tilts his head from side to side when he's listening to me. I'd probably even miss him pulling my knickers from the laundry basket. Life would be so much duller without Dennis. Of all the dubious decisions I've made in my life, this was not one of them. I'm so glad I went to see him that day, my puppy with the world map on his back.

18 MAY

Mum and I take Beano and Dennis to Goodwoof, a dog festival in Sussex. It's Glastonbury, essentially, but for 12,000 dogs and their owners. There's a dog tarot reader, dog yoga, a grooming salon, sheepdog trials, and a lido ('Fido's Lido'), where Beano and Dennis splash around together. Afterwards, Mum and I visit the crystal healer, a woman called Yvette, who's sitting in a teepee.

'Does Dennis have any issues?' Yvette asks.

'Recall could be better,' I reply, whereupon she rubs a piece of rose quartz up and down his back, then hands me a little bag of both rose quartz and amethyst to take home, which will apparently help calm him. 'But don't place them in his bed, in case he ingests them,' Yvette warns.

Later, on stage alongside Jodie Kidd and Tom Felton (Draco Malfoy from *Harry Potter*), I help judge the best-dressed competition. First prize, we decide, should go to a pair of rescue dogs – Audrey and Margarita – both wearing a pair of flower garlands around their necks, with second prize to a small sausage dog called Winston, in the same stripy shirt as his owner, and third prize to a scruffy terrier not unlike Dennis, called Roger.

Dennis does a wee under my chair, either because he drunk too much water beforehand, or due to stage fright.

19 MAY

I find the small bag that contained the crystals on my kitchen floor. The little amethyst stone is lying nearby, but the rose quartz has mysteriously vanished. Wonder if it'll have any noticeable effect.

20 MAY

'Any sign of the rose quartz?' texts Mum.

'No,' I text back, as I watch Dennis try to catch the same fly he's been after for twenty minutes, batting the kitchen doors with his paws and jumping in the air with his mouth open, 'but he seems fine.'

21 MAY

Progress on the training front in the park. We walked past a goose this morning and he didn't even look at it.

'GOOD BOY,' I said, loud enough that Martians in outer space could have heard it.

23 MAY

Sussex. Mum's taken the old lawn mower to the skip, so there's now a deckchair strapped to the front of the chicken gate with a bungee to stop Dennis getting in. The three remaining chickens – Jane, Lizzy and Mary – cluck to one another like old fishwives behind the fence while Dennis watches with interest from the other side. I sit in the evening sun with a glass of wine, ensuring he doesn't creep too close and issuing the occasional warning: 'Dennis …' On hearing this, he looks away from the chickens, pretending that he's entirely uninterested in them, and sniffs a flower.

Mum's inside, making bread. The perfect, peaceful, entirely unremarkable evening. Her recent MRI result was clear. No cancer growing back. 'Good brain,' her longstanding oncologist has said, a phrase that Mum, my siblings and I keep repeating to one another with joy: 'Good brain!'

Good brain. The best brain. A medical marvel.

24 MAY

Bank holiday weekend. Take Dennis for a long walk on the South Downs and come across two middle-aged men with poles and large rucksacks walking the same stretch. One of them is blind and explains that he's walking the 100-mile path, from Winchester to Eastbourne, to raise money for the Guide Dog Association. He nearly brought his guide dog, he says, a German shepherd, but worried that the flinty ground would be too hard for her feet. I look at Dennis, picking his way along the chalk path, and feel guilty because Eve and I have planned a two-day walk along the same stretch over the next couple of days, and Mum is already worrying that it'll be too much for him.

Wonder if I should have invested in a doggy rucksack. Too late now.

25 MAY

Eve and I begin walking just south of Lewes, Dennis bounding along the path in front of us. Stop for lunch at a pub in the idyllic village of Firle – little brick cottages festooned with roses, pink foxgloves waving in the flowerbeds – and inspect the map over a glass of rosé. Continue for another three hours along the chalky path afterwards, with sensational views of lush green Sussex fields on one side and the sea on another. We chat along the way, about her marriage, and my latest feelings about whether or not to have children, and what cake we'd most like for tea from the approaching café. That's the joy of an old friendship – you can move from ovaries to carrot cake in a single sentence.

Stop for the night at a new, dog-friendly hotel in another bucolic village. The hotel has a croquet lawn, bedrooms with expensive wallpaper and pretty, upholstered headboards. Eve and I borrow a pair of flip-flops from the spa for dinner because we're sick of wearing our walking boots, then order a bottle of Sussex champagne to celebrate our ten-mile hike. Dennis sleeps between us, stretched out on the banquette.

She asks how I'm feeling about the director and Spain, in two weeks' time.

How *am* I feeling? I don't entirely know. I want to be with someone, I tell her. Ironically, that was one of the helpful lessons that emerged from my relationship with Mike; for years, I'd viewed wanting to be with someone as a weakness, that it denoted some form of insecurity, as almost shameful. Now I know it can just be really, really lovely. But I still don't know if that someone's the director.

'Don't overthink it,' she warns, before twirling her hand in the air like a flamenco dancer to summon a waiter. 'Just go, see, have a nice time. Now, let's have another bottle.'

'How are his little legs?' Mum texts later, as we stagger back to our hotel room, Dennis half-asleep in my arms.

'Fine!' I reply, once I've lowered him onto the bed.

26 MAY

Unfortunately, there was a large poo on the new hotel carpet when I woke up this morning. 'Could be from a walking boot?' Eve muses, frowning at it. I dampen a towel and try to remove the stain, then we check out and decide not to mention anything.

We embark on the Seven Sisters, the cliff path that stretches towards Beachy Head. Very hilly, very windy. I keep Dennis on the lead but see various other dog owners let theirs run close to the edge, where there's a 500-foot drop to the rocks below. Nutters.

Dennis is so tired by the final ascent that I keep picking him up and carrying him. Probably won't tell Mum this.

Reward him with a piece of celebratory burger in the pub at the end. On the drive back to London, Eve and I are so exhausted we can barely speak. Dennis sleeps on her lap for the entire trip.

'Love you,' I say, hugging her on my driveway, before she heads back to hers.

'Love you both,' she says, pulling back and gently touching Dennis on the nose. 'See you after Spain.'

28 MAY

Fall into step with a dog walker in the park who has two elderly schnauzers on the lead, Elvis and Priscilla.

'He's only one?' he exclaims, when I tell him Dennis's age. 'Blimey. I have 'em all – small dogs, big dogs, young dogs, old dogs – and you've got yourself a little gem here.'

On the way home, Dennis slightly ruins this by swallowing a chicken bone from the pavement, and then spends the evening walking very slowly around the garden, occasionally stopping and straining, like a woman in labour.

But mostly, I know I have got myself a little gem. I can't believe it, sometimes, when I look at him and think 'He's mine', when he jumps up on my bed in the mornings and spins a few times before curling into a ball against my feet. He's mine. I found him.

If I think back to when he arrived, to the moments I didn't think I could do it, to the moments when I dared to imagine giving him back, I now feel overwhelmed with relief that I kept him. If I hadn't found Dennis, my relationship with Mike might have continued for longer. At the time of the break-up, in the autumn, I couldn't bear the idea that Dennis was the catalyst, but nine months on I couldn't be more grateful.

He has saved me in a way, from a potentially more complicated life, from trouble down the road.

29 MAY

I'm thrashing around with the Victorian novel at the kitchen table when Dennis comes in from the garden and jumps up and looks at me imploringly, his front paws on my thigh.

'I can't come and play,' I tell him. 'I have to work so I can keep you in expensive biscuits.'

He doesn't budge, so I lift him up and he settles down on my legs with a happy sigh. This means I have to tap at the keyboard with my forearms lifted above him and my hands bent down at an angle, as if Frankenstein's monster is learning to type.

On all those posters about correct workplace posture, I've never once seen a dog on anyone's lap, but it is companionable, his stomach rising and falling with mine. Make a mental note to book an osteopath appointment, because my shoulders feel hunched writing like this. But I still don't want to move him. My little hero.

30 MAY

Dennis and I catch the train to Islington for coffee with a friend. I feel something like the pressing of an old bruise as we slide through Hoxton, Mike's stop, and hold my breath in case I see a familiar head above the tourists and 20-somethings in big earphones.

Afterwards, we catch the bus to Highgate. Endearingly, the director made lamb patties yesterday to try them in advance of our dinner tonight. A dress rehearsal, he says, to check they were good enough. I sit on a stool with a glass of rosé while he makes a salad, and then we eat in his garden, fairy lights on overhead as it gets dark. Noticing a suspicious lack of Dennis, I go inside and find him asleep, curled into a ball on the director's bed.

'The baby's asleep,' I tell him, settling back down on the sofa in his garden. Although only for a few minutes, because then we decide to go in and watch our favourite quiz show. Romance, I'm learning, can be quieter and less dramatic than the poets and films would have us believe.

31 MAY

I wake up next to the director and take out my earplugs. We managed a night sleeping beside one another.

'Did I snore?' he checks.

'*Yes*,' I reply emphatically, 'but I slept. A bit.'

We have tea in bed, Dennis lying between us, then walk through Highgate Wood to a café for breakfast. As we're going on holiday in less than a week, we talk about the beaches in Spain, and the restaurants we might go to, and our attitudes towards suncream (mine quite strict; his less so), and the books we're taking. 'And I think there probably is a conversation to be had about exclusivity,' he says quietly, and I nod because there is, although I still don't know the answer to that question. Maybe it'll become clear when we're there.

'See you at the airport,' he says, before kissing me outside the Tube station.

'See you at the airport,' I repeat, squeezing his hand.

The Northern Line is so packed that I lift Dennis onto my lap to avoid him being trodden on. I have him, I think, no matter who else may come in or out of my life. I have him even if I don't have children. I have him, hopefully for a good while yet, so long as we can avoid any further dramas with cliffs, ponds, rivers, and fast-moving vehicles. I'm so very, very lucky that I have Dennis.

It's not quite the love story I envisaged this time a year ago when I was longing to collect him and bring him home. But it's a love story all the same.

Acknowledgements

It was summer 2023. Lisa Milton, my brilliant publisher at HQ, emailed suggesting a meeting. 'Could we possibly make it a breakfast meeting?' I replied, explaining that I had a new puppy and he couldn't be left alone for very long, but that I could dart to London Bridge and back for a coffee and a croissant.

I arrived feeling like a harried new mother – hair unbrushed, shirt probably done up with the wrong buttons, puppy drool on my trousers, and bags the size of a bus under my eyes from all the sleepless nights.

We chatted about this and that, then Lisa mentioned an idea she'd had for a book called *The Year of the Dog*, a humorous account of my first year with the dog I'd christened Dennis. Having never written a non-fiction book before, I was intrigued but unsure. How could I write a book about my dog when I was – back then – worrying that I couldn't even look after him properly? What would this book look like?

My first thank you, therefore, goes to Lisa for being such a champion and for having this idea. It's a slightly different book, I think, to the one we first envisaged, given the various ups and downs of the past year. But I couldn't be more grateful that you were, and remain, so encouraging.

To Rachael Kilduff and Danielle Pender for all your editing work, and to the wider HQ team, thank you for being equally wonderful, for putting up with emails at strange times of day and night, for making the right noises whenever I sent you yet another picture of Dennis, for looking after this book so carefully. Because it's more personal than anything I've written before, I'm even more grateful to you all, too.

To Zebedee Helm, king among illustrators, thank you for lunch that day in Lewes, held because I insisted you needed to meet Dennis 'to really understand his character'. Thank you for drawing such beautiful images, and for also tolerating the number of photos I sent you. Your illustrations are going to make me smile forever. Especially the one of the poor birder being peed on. Thanks, too, to Fi Cotter-Craig and Cesca Major for introducing us.

To my agent Georgina Capel, and sidekick Simon Shaps, thank you both for being so stupendously supportive. A number of neurotic emails went your way, too, so actually it's thanks and apologies in equal measure.

Thank you to Lorraine Flood for breeding Dennis in the first place. I will feel lucky forever that I came to see fat, fluffy baby Dennis and his siblings on that hot day in May 2023, and returned a month later to scoop him up in a Quavers box.

To my fellow dog owners and walkers of Crystal Palace, thank you for so much advice – on training (still a work in progress, if I'm honest), the best treats, the best toys, the best treatment for blocked anal glands, and for plenty of discussion about the pros and cons of castration. You have enlivened my mornings (and afternoons) no end. Special mention to Uncle Larry, for looking after Dennis from time to time, for making me laugh, and for sage relationship advice.

To my family and friends, thank you for all being there, and for allowing Dennis to trash your carpets and sofas, too. Also, for never complaining when I asked if we could meet in a dog-friendly restaurant. Mum, thank you especially, not only for allowing me to talk about your story in here, but also for loving and looking after Dennis like a grandchild. I'm so sorry about all the chewed hairbrushes. And the chicken.

Penultimately, to the director – thank you for being such a superhero. For the weekends, and the weekdays, for the theatre trips, for the oysters, for the long voice notes, for making my birthday not feel lonely, for the weird-flavoured crisps and my second-hand book. Thank you for also loving Dennis. You made all the difference. And I really am still sorry about the loo handle.

Finally, to Dennis. Thank you for making me see that I don't necessarily need a baby for my life to feel full.